Hired 2.0

Recruiting
Exceptional
Talent

at the
Speed of
Light

Dr. Denis Cauvier

Other Books by Dr. Denis Cauvier:
- How to Hire the Right Person
- How To Keep Your Staff Productive & Happy
- Achieve It! A Personal Success Journal
- The ABC's of Making Money (co-authored by Alan Lysaght)
- Attracting, Selecting and Retaining GREAT People
- The ABC's of Making Money 4 Teens (co-authored by Alan Lysaght)
- 101 Low Cost/ High Impact Recruiting Methods

First Edition, First Printing - Copyright © 2010 by DAX Enterprises International Inc.

Publication design & layout by MORRgraphics Inc.
Back cover photo by Emily Raglan
Printed in Canada by Dollco Printing (Ottawa) Limited
10 9 8 7 6 5 4 3 2 1

Library and Archives Canada Cataloguing in Publication

Cauvier, Denis L., 1963-Hired 2.0: recruiting exceptional people at the speed of light/Denis Cauvier.

ISBN 978-0-9736514-2-3

1. Employees--Recruiting. 2.   Employee selection. 3.   Social media. I. Title.

HF5549.5.R44C358 2010   658.3'11   C2009-906652-1

This book is dedicated to

Debbie

A beacon of strength,
A model of integrity,
A wise and compassionate critic,
A loving, full-time mother,

My life partner.

Acknowledgements

Interdependence trumps independence.

This work, like all of my books is a synergistic product of many minds. I have gained so many insights and gems of wisdom from numerous colleagues, hundreds of clients and countless attendees at my various presentations around the world. Some specific people that I would like to acknowledge;

To Shane Gibson the co-author of *Sociable! How social media marketing is turning sales and marketing upside-down*, who has been instrumental in dragging me into the 21st Century.

To Bill Gibson my first business mentor who has shared so much with me over the years.

To George Foster for the world class book cover design.

To Cindy Morris for all her formatting and layout work over various projects.

To Lillian Cauvier and Alan Lysaght for editing the manuscript.

To Emily Raglan for the "non-corporate" photo shoot

To the wonderful management and staff at Tryp Resorts International for providing the perfect atmosphere for my writing retreat.

To the awesome team at Speakers Spotlight, I am honoured to be represented by the best speaker's bureau in North America.

To my parents who are such passionate cheerleaders of my efforts.

To my two wonderful daughters for bringing so much light into my life.

To Debbie, my life partner for "sticking around" lol

Foreword

As a social media evangelist, speaker and author I read a lot of books and attend numerous seminars on the topic of using social media and social networks to attract talent. Very few authors and presenters actually have a strong footing in historical best practices as well as a grasp of Web 2.0. In this book you will find proven strategies for hiring using the most current and up-to-date methodologies and social technologies.

Before I go any further though, we need to look at why most companies need to update the way they recruit and attract talent:

With employees, customers and stakeholders equipped with technology that allows for mass collaboration and rapid communication we as leaders need to understand how to harness this technology and the crowds we are connected to.

Today's workplace is not a homogeneous one. As leaders we have to lead teams that are made up of Baby Boomers, Generation X and Generation Y. This coupled with diverse cultures and values in the workplace make leading both exciting and challenging. We can't recruit our Generation Y talent the way we recruited our leaders of yesteryear.

In the past there were few media available to consume or advertise on. We had mainstream print, niche periodicals, radio and television. If we were recruiting new talent we would use these mediums combined with job fairs, presentations, and our personal networks. A job posting on a local newspaper in the classifieds, combined with a radio spot used to do the trick.

Today, our potential employees get their information and news from their friends on sites like Twitter. They peruse Craigslist. org and LinkedIn.com for job opportunities, and they have over 200 channels on TV to watch. Marketing to this fragmented demographic using old-fashioned advertising is difficult.

If you do manage to reach the right candidate they have already read blogs about your company by former employees, they've read your most recent press releases and they have visited your personal LinkedIn profile to see who will be interviewing them. In fact they're getting ready to interview you!

This is not a trend that will fade, it is a shift in the way people network, process information and communicate with one another. We are living in a transparent world, where authenticity and purpose are valued by today's new league of employees more than dollars or slick logos. For the recruiters and companies that get it this, there's a huge opportunity.

In his book Hired 2.0, Denis takes his 20 plus years as a recruiter/ consultant/ speaker and best-selling author and outlines a step-by-step process and set of principles that will help you succeed in this new environment. Before you spend another dollar on recruiting efforts, invest a few hours in reading this book, implement the process and you will attract the hard to find talent that you are looking for.

Shane Gibson
Co-author of *Sociable!*
@shanegibson

Message from Dr. Denis Cauvier

As the song goes, "the times they are a-changin'", there is no denying that the technology has affected virtually every facet of business over the past decade. The internet has evolved to what has been termed Web 2.0. The implications are revolutionizing the way we do business. With social media sites like Twitter, LinkedIn and Facebook popping up daily recruiters have immediate interactive opportunities to promote their vacancies but also to access prospective hires. As new fibre optic lines shoot electrons around the planet approaching the speed of light, tapping into the global talent pool through "word of mouth" via social media sites is becoming the new recruiting norm and it's happening at the "speed of light"

I have divided this book into three parts. *The introduction* depicts the current and most major indicators predicting what the labour market will look like in the next few years. Part one addresses the 10 key employee experiences that an organization must excel at in order to be recognized as an employer of choice, greatly affecting it's brand and it's referability. Part two focuses on using social media recruiting to identify, engage, recruit, and pre-screen hard to reach talent, with numerous examples of successful employers provided.

A critical point is not to forget all the traditional recruiting methods that continue to serve you well, but rather to supplement and re-enforce your organization's brand while broadcasting recruiting messages via social media marketing.

Introduction

*I*t's fascinating to explore beyond the pervasive negative economic news that has overwhelmed us during the past year and a half. Companies are shedding jobs, people are spending less, the US mortgage and housing market experienced a major crisis, Wall Street and the North American Auto sector required massive bailouts, America has mortgaged future generations to China and the gloom and doom continued. It is always interesting to me when the media reports "averages". For example, recently all the media was covering how car sales in North America were down an average of 38%. Although that was the extent of the coverage on the story by most media outlets, it did not tell the entire story. To get the complete picture of auto sales in North America at that time one would have to examine how each car company fared. The big three did poorer than 38%, Korean and Japanese were down between 12% to 26%, while VW and Audi were up 2% in the middle of what most economists have called "the worst economic recession since the great depression." This example reinforces to me the dangers of over reading into averages. Here is another way to view averages, if you are average you are the best of the worst or the worst of the best!

Another way to see the folly in putting too much weight on averages alone is to consider this situation. Imagine that you are at home in your kitchen, you remove your shoes and your socks, you then place one of your bare feet into the hot oven while the other foot goes into the freezer... on average you are comfortable. I know that is a silly example but it does serve to remind us to examine both the highs and the lows that contribute to the composition of an average.

It is also interesting to note that the organizations that buy into the negative news and focus solely on the average, find themselves being average and using the recession as an excuse for doing so poorly. Winning companies decide that they will take charge of their own economy by being better than average with the caliber of the products and services they offer, their innovative cost reduction methods, their levels of service excellence and their ability to keep their people productive and happy.

I have during the height of the recession been doing several separate speaking tours to some of the hardest hit areas; Detroit, Windsor/ Sarnia corridor, Las Vegas, LA and several cities in Florida. No, I was not speaking on the home foreclosure market or creative job finding skills. I was speaking to groups and networks of employers that despite the current economic situations were **growing** and were **having challenges finding great people**. During my various tours, many business owners and senior leaders mentioned that the downsizing of staff was really the right sizing because it provided the opportunity to get rid of poor performers. As the economy is picking up and will continue to recover they were all interested in finding the best possible people. They were not interested in people who are unemployed. These savvy employers were seeking passive job seekers, the ones who are gainfully employed but are not fully satisfied with their current job and or employers. Today's best candidates, even when they are not actively looking for new jobs, are constantly renewing their networks and online profiles and often are seeking to establish themselves as influencers in their industry.

Recently, there have been several national surveys conducted to determine the major concerns of senior leaders from both the private and public sectors. The listing below illustrates the most common concerns that are keeping these leaders awake at night:

Executive Insomnia

- 10 % Competition
- 29 % Economic Issues
- 22 % Profits/Cash-Flow
- 25 % Future of Company
- 31 % H.R. Issues (Recruiting, engaging and retaining staff)

Sober Economic Projections

There is an alarming fact that many people are unaware of that is a top concern of recruiters. Canada will not have enough workers within a few years and the available workforce will lack the skills and knowledge that the global economy demands. The specific skills that will be lacking are: soft skills, interpersonal skills, literary skills and core occupational skills. There are a number of pressure points that currently affect and will continue to affect the labour market into the future.

Labour Market Challenges for 2010 & Beyond

- 2010 Olympics & oil gas sector
- Fast food workers in Alberta starting at + $ 13.25/ hr
- BC & Saskatchewan targeting local labour
- Increase labour costs
- Rapidly changing technology
- Increased pressures of transparency & accountability
- Changing legislation
- Increased client expectations
- Relative low national rate of unemployment yet pockets of high unemployment
- More high tech workers in Ottawa than federal workers
- Devaluation of canadian dollar
- 9.8% national high school drop out rate
- Continued shift from rural to urban living
- Last decade Canadian labour force had 2% new entrants/year
- Next decade decline of 6% entrants/ year
- Critical skilled labour shortages
- 44% of all "master" level trade people to retire over next 5 years
- 47% of middle & senior level public service workers eligible for retirement within 7 years
- Shortage of 520,000 immigrants/ year to meet projected labour needs

The bottom line is that the competition for labour will increase and employers will be faced with a critical decision to either lower their standards for new hires (like the cartoon below illustrates) or to become an employer of choice where many great passive job seekers apply for positions within the company.

Of course the problem with lowering standards is that you end up hiring people you don't really want. They can be less productive, less client oriented, more accident prone, more wasteful, have a negative attitude that either pulls down the rest of the team or encourages the best performers to become passive job seekers and look for better opportunities elsewhere.

> *"Most people do not leave an average paying job because of the nature of the pay; rather they leave due to the nature of the people they have to work with."*
> **Dr. Denis Cauvier**

Organizations that don't invest sufficiently in the areas of attracting, selecting, hiring, developing, engaging and retaining the best talent will suffer the high costs of employee turnover.

"Experience? Are you kidding? I've had 12 jobs this year alone!"

   With all of the above mentioned labour challenges in mind smart employers are investing heavily in trying to attract, select, hire, develop, engage and retain the best talent. These organizations understand that their best strategic advantage is their people. Recruiters have always sought the fastest, cheapest methods to increase both quantity and quality of applicants. Tapping into the global talent pool by combining "word of mouth recruiting" at the "speed of light" is the most cost effective way to win the battle for talent.

   Using social media recruiting can level the playing field so that smaller firms can find exceptional talent as effectively as the Fortune 500 ones do. Social media recruiting serves not only to greatly expand the potential pool of applicants, but to also serve as a useful part of the pre-screening process. A recent social media survey of 100 hiring managers at small, mid-size and large companies found they used the following social media marketing to find talent for job openings:

- 66 % LinkedIn
- 23 % Facebook
- 16 % Twitter.

The same companies were also asked how many of them research job candidates prior to making a job offer on the following sites:

- 75% LinkedIn
- 48% Facebook
- 26% Twitter.

Another recently released survey backing up the position that more recruiters are turning to social media for talent was conducted by the recruitment solutions provider Jobvite. Their second annual Social Recruitment Survey showed that employers are more and more extensively recruiting on social networks, such as Facebook and Twitter. It also shows that the companies appear more satisfied with these types of recruits versus the ones they find solely from job boards or more traditional recruitment channels. In fact, due to these satisfaction levels companies are likely to invest more in social media recruiting in the near future, while trimming down their spending with traditional channels and search firms. Here are some specific statistics uncovered:

- 76% of companies surveyed plan to invest more in employee referrals
- 72% plan to invest more in recruiting through social networks
- 80% of companies are planning to use social networks to find or attract candidates
- LinkedIn use grew from 80% in 2008 to 95% in 2008
- Facebook use grew from 36% in 2008 to 59% in 2009
- Twitter ranked third at 42%

One very interesting notation from the Jobvite survey was "employee referrals are still the most highly rated sources in terms of quality of candidates generated". I will focus a great deal of part one of this book on how to create the right conditions / experiences so that your job openings are referable.

One simple way to look at what constitutes being an employer of choice is when 100% of the entire team, naturally without being asked, acts as informal recruiters by spreading the news of the job opportunity to their contacts and by making referrals.

> *"Social media enables me to build that initial network and make connections thousands of times faster than picking up a phone book and a phone calling into my client's competitors. I also put calls out on Twitter when I have a position to fill...this basically enables my network to identify candidates for me that I would otherwise not had access to. Facebook serves a similar purpose. It is a rare case that I would be forced to actually advertise a position. Generally speaking, using my methods, I can have fully screened candidates for a client within two to three days. This is weeks faster than other agencies who use no social media and choose to advertise only."*
>
> **Jennifer Wojcik, CEO of YouGuru LLC**

Part 1:

Being referable – what are the speed of light conversations about your organization – an "inside-out model"

'Becoming an employer of choice', within HR circles this term has virtually become cliché… it's easier said than done… Countless organizations call themselves an employer of choice. They have lofty vision and mission statements expanding on how their staff is their most valuable asset, yet they continue to suffer with costly high employee turnover, low levels of staff engagement and costly recruitment campaigns with poor results. I believe the answer to all of this is the following model:

Organizations routinely spend millions of dollars on advertising a message to attempt to create a brand. Unfortunately, all of this money spent goes down the drain if someone's experience is less than what the "brand message" promised. In reality, a company's brand is what other's (employees and outsiders) say it is, not what their paid advertising claims it to be. Your brand is really the culmination of all the conversations in your universe that are being held pertaining to your organization. The single biggest factor that drives these conversations is the type of service experience that each individual has with your company. As indicated by the **Recruiting Exceptional Talent from the Inside-Out** model, here is a way to view the various players in your organization's universe:

S taff
E xecutives
R ecruiters
V isitors both customers and browsers (in person and online)
I nvestors that own shares in the company
C orrespondents/ media reporters
E veryone else that comprises your company's universe

The inside-out perspective of this model refers to the fact that staff has the greatest influence on a company's ability to recruit exceptional talent. That investing in your current staff is the most important place to start. Happy, productive and highly engaged employees will want to make referrals when provided with the opportunity to do so. How a company's employees feel about their job, their co-workers, their customers and their employer greatly affects the level of SERVICE they provide to the rest of your universe. The type of experience each person has directly affects the conversations they will have with others. These conversations can be at the water cooler, the local coffee shop, or much more commonly today in cyberspace via social networks. Ultimately it's these conversations that determine your brand.

Lessons from Customer Service

Imagine seeing lots of very compelling ads for a new local restaurant. The ads promise great food served by gracious service professionals in a welcoming atmosphere. You and a few friends decide to check out the new eatery. Imagine receiving very poor service and undercooked food and when trying to explain the problem to the waiter he becomes rude. Upon paying for the meal the manager says, "I hope you will encourage your friends and family to come check us out, and if they do we will give you a coupon for a free appetizer." You most likely will not take the manager up on his offer. This example is similar to how many companies execute their Employee Referral Programs. They encourage employees to recruit friends and family members to work for an organization that is less-than-stellar and they then offer a token referral bonus. It should come as no surprise that this approach to employee referrals yields little to no results.

It is all About the Experience

If you want a more successful Employee Referral Program, you first need to make sure you are giving your employees something to brag about. The following slogan applies to both the world of customer service as well as creating an organization that employees will be proud to share with others.

> *"People will go to where they are invited, will stay when they are appreciated and will tell others when encouraged to do so!"*
> **Bill Gibson, professional speaker/author**

To turn a workforce into a team of recruiters, take an honest look at the work experience delivered.

Create the Right Experience, They Will Talk

Asking questions about the work experience delivered to employees will help design the kind of experience that employees want to talk about. They will WANT to tell their contacts because they will feel so lucky, and they know how exceptional their employer is. They will WANT to give the people they care about and respect an opportunity to be as lucky as they are.

Not only does creating such a satisfying, motivating, inspiring work experience turn a workforce into a band of head-hunters, it also improves morale, productivity, engagement and customer service quality. This is not a "nice to do if we had the time" project. Doing this well has far reaching implications for the very sources of your financial viability.

Are your job openings and your organization referable?

It all boils down to your current and former employee's reactions to 10 key experiences:

1. Recruiting, Pre-selection, Job Offer and Welcoming Package Experience
2. Onboarding- Pulling out the red carpet Experience
3. Interpersonal Relations and Communications Experience
4. Training & Development Experience
5. Receiving Informal Feedback and Formal Performance Evaluation Experience
6. Employee Level of Satisfaction Experience
7. The Boss Experience
8. Employee Recognition Experience
9. Employee Referral Experience
10. Employee Exiting Experience

"You get the best out of others when you give the best of yourself."

Harvey Firestone

1. Recruiting, pre-selection, job offer and welcoming package experience

Are your recruiting messages consistent with your organization's core values and mission? Do your recruiting efforts attract quality job seekers?

Given today's competitive labour market some companies will settle for "a warm body". The danger with this approach is that by lowering recruiting standards, a company is ultimately weakening their labour force. The cost of employee turnover is very expensive when factoring all costs of hiring, training and developing new staff. These costs directly affect the bottom line performance of a company.

Is your pre-screening and interviewing process applicant-friendly? Does it communicate a favourable impression and reinforce the decision to apply for work at your company?

Do you conduct a site tour and review of the job duties with all short listed candidates as part of the selection process prior to making the hiring decision?

The rationale for investing in this small additional effort is that it provides the applicant with realistic expectations of the job while providing you the opportunity to gauge their reaction to the work environment. If the person is not likely to "work out" it is best to know this prior to hiring and orientating them.

Are you able to screen job applicants quickly in order to make firm offers?

The key is to not lose good applicants to the competition by taking too long to act.

Do you provide a written job offer detailing the job position, start date, wage information and who, when and where to report to on the first day?

A new employee may benefit from reading information about the organization prior to beginning their new job. Determine the information that is appropriate to send to the new employee for review prior to the first day on the new job. Identify which information is simply informational and which requires action by the new employee. At the end of this section is the "Customize Your Own Orientation Content Checklist." This checklist is a tool that can be photocopied and used by your Human Resources department to create an orientation process uniquely tailored to your company's needs.

A welcome package could include the following:

_____	Welcome letters
_____	Employee handbook
_____	Relocation kit
_____	Local area maps
_____	Parking areas; sticker or pass
_____	Transit route information
_____	Supervisor's name and location
_____	Copy of job description
_____	Normal work hours
_____	Uniform-ordering information
_____	Dress-code information
_____	Safety information
_____	Benefit-plan information
_____	Food handling practices
_____	Organizational chart
_____	Organizational newsletter
_____	Length of probationary period
_____	Union information
_____	Community links (churches, restaurants, schools, health-care facilities, etc.)

2. On-boarding- pulling out the red carpet experience

Employee on-boarding is the process of welcoming new recruits and helping them become happy, productive fully engaged workers. On-boarding should be seen as a process and not as a single event. On-boarding is not to be confused with new employee orientation. Orientation is an important phase within the overall employee on-boarding process. The on-boarding process consists of the following phases:

1. Recruiting & Pre-screening – Testing The Waters
2. Job Offer & Welcome Package
3. First Day – First Impression
4. First Week – Getting Acquainted
5. First 30 Days – Settling In & Avoiding "Hires Regret"
6. First 60 Days – Adjusting & Becoming Fully Engaged
7. Maintenance and further relationship development

Benefits of Employee On-boarding

Employee turnover costs employers a tremendous amount of time, energy and money. In fact it has been identified that the largest proportion of employee turnover occurs in the first 60 days of employment.

7 Common Mistakes to Avoid

1. "Mind-Stuffing" trying to cram 20 hours of information into 4 mind-numbing hours.
2. "Fake it till you make it" unprepared, disorganized and frenzied process. The reality of business today is that everything is at a fast pace. That being said, the notion of "go slower, to go faster" applies here. A formal orientation process should be well thought out and should include clear instruction regarding safety and productivity expectations. Care taken at this stage will result in a shorter training cycle, less waste and increased production.
3. "Like watching paint dry" hours of data dumps, form-filing marathons and "death by training videos."

4. "Sink or swim" throwing a new employee into the fray without support and coaching. Many employers have some form of a "buddy system" to assist the new recruits. The key to fully capitalizing on a buddy system is to ensure that the right people are selected as buddies, that they receive training in their roles as buddies and perhaps most importantly, that they actually want to be a buddy.

5. "No news, is good news", no formal/informal "check-in" with new employee to gauge their development.

6. "One-size fits all"–not accounting for an individual's age, gender or culture.

7. "It is not my job" to welcome a new employee.

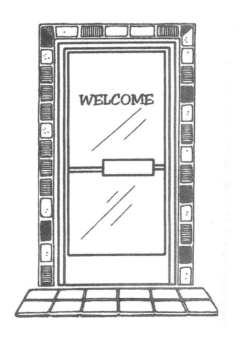

12 Disciplines of an Effective Employee On-boarding Process

1. New employees feel welcomed and valued.
2. New employees feel proud that they made the right decision to join the company.
3. New employees feel that they are part of the "big picture".
4. Recognition and rewarding of new employees' contributions.
5. Collect and share company stories to make learning points memorable.
6. Make the experience interesting and interactive for new employees.
7. Design the process from the new employees' perspective.
8. Select the most effective time and method of communicating orientation information.
9. Deliver your program in bite sized chunks of information.
10. Have an effective buddy system as part of your orientation program.
11. Get early evaluation of orientation from new employee and supervisor.
12. Remember, leadership is everything. Ensure that managers, supervisors and buddies have the needed training for their portion of the on-boarding process and they also have a positive attitude.

Your On-boarding Process Should Address These Issues:

7 Most Common Concerns of New Employees
1. Is this the right job for me?
2. Will I be able to do the job?
3. Am I "in over my head"?
4. What will my supervisor/lead hand be like to work with?
5. Will I fit in and be welcomed?
6. I'm younger/older/or I am from a different cultural background. Will I be understood and respected?
7. The pace here is so busy. Will someone actually be able to take the time to train me?

20 Common Questions from New Employees
1. What is this new job really about?
2. How well will I be able to handle the physical, repetitive nature of the work?
3. How well will I cope with the cold or hot production area temperatures?
4. Where do I report to first?
5. What are the priorities?
6. What do I need to know to become productive?
7. Will I receive enough training to keep me safe?
8. Where do I go when I need help or more information?
9. What am I going to do for lunch? Will I be alone?
10. Who are the other people in my department, and what do they do?
11. How can I best "fit-in" with my co-workers?
12. Who has the right information when information conflicts?
13. Who do I go to for answers to problems?
14. How will I remember all this new information?
15. How does the phone work? How are messages handled?
16. Where is the rest room, lunch room, break room, changing rooms and lockers?
17. Will clothing and personal protection equipment (safety boots, hard hat, ear protectors etc.) be provided for me?
18. What are the "unwritten rules"?
19. How and when do I get paid?
20. How available is my boss or supervisor when I need help?

A new employee's first impression of the job, co-workers, supervisor and the company will be for the most part developed during the first week on the job. New employees start a job with enthusiasm and positive energy, it is critical to keep this attitude. Adopt the mind set of pulling out the red carpet by welcoming the new employee to the team. This is the best time to ensure that they start off on the right foot by covering all of the basics listed on the Onboarding Planner Tool found on page 27. A benefit of an effective orientation is that the new employee's decision to join with your company has been re-enforced so that they feel that they have made the right decision. This is a very smart investment of time to reduce staff turnover.

Common Emotions Felt by New Employees during Successful On-boarding

- Welcome
- Safe
- Important
- Proud
- Happy
- Confident
- Respected

Common Emotions Felt by New Employees during Unsuccessful On-boarding

- Confused
- Frustrated
- Worried
- Bored
- Nervous
- Afraid
- Upset

Note: If new people experience these emotions they will be on their way to becoming disengaged with their work and the company, which leads to poor levels of productivity, and higher rates of turnover.

Whose Job is it anyway?

Leadership is everything – Senior executives need to define and model the vision that all staff – especially new employees – are welcomed, supported, encouraged and developed.

Human Resources – It is a common misconception that it is solely the role of Human Resources to help new employees through the on-boarding process. Human Resources should be seen as the support mechanism that helps co-ordinate all departments in welcoming new hires.

Supervisors – Because they have the most daily direct contact and communications with their teammates, it is vital that supervisors have the training, skills, support, resources and positive attitude towards their role in welcoming and developing new employees.

Quality Assurance Personnel & Trainers – These people work with employees on the line and have a great opportunity to ensure high production and safety standards as well as to model and encourage high standards in dealing with co-workers.

Peers – It is important that the entire organization is part of the support system for all new staff and of particular importance is the role provided by buddies.

Individual – Lastly, we must also recognize that it is up to the new employee to take the initiative to capitalize on the opportunities that the on-boarding process and new job offers them.

Sample Welcome Letter from Human Resources

[Today's Date]

[Employee's Name]
[Employee's Address]

Dear [Employee's Name]:
I want to formally confirm your acceptance of our employment offer to begin work on [start date] as [job title]. When you arrive at [arrival time & date], please come to my office in the Human Resources department at [building and room number].

Your first morning will be spent with one of our Human Resources representatives. Enclosed are some materials that can be helpful for you to review prior to your first day of work. There are also some forms that you can complete and bring with you on your first day.

We will help you enrol in our payroll and benefit systems. To prepare you to make some of those decisions, please review the forms and pamphlets enclosed. We will also go on a facility tour before you report to work on your first afternoon.

You will be our guest for lunch on your first day. The welcoming committee is looking forward to meeting you.

If you have questions before [start date], please give me a call at [Human Resources manager's phone number].

Sincerely,

[Human Resources Manager's Name]
[Human Resources Manager's Title]

Onboarding Planning Tool

This tool suggests the main topics that should be covered with the new employee during the orientation period. It makes sense in many cases to space out the majority of items covered during the orientation over a period of several days, and the remaining items over the next few months, which provides time for the new employee to both actively work in the capacity for what they were hired for and allows time to absorb the information being covered during the orientation.

Customize Your Own Orientation Content Checklist

The "Orientation Content Checklist" is designed to assist those who design and conduct new employee orientation. The checklist recommends a comprehensive list of topics, to help the new employee function productively. To avoid overwhelming the new employee on the first day, it is necessary to identify the best *timing* for each item. Information is most beneficial when it is given to the new employee closest to the time when it is to be used.

Next, identify who is the best source of information. Some information is best learned and retained if the employee "discovers" it himself or herself. Most standardized information is best delivered by the Human Resources function. Information that varies from one department to another is best given by a supervisor. A buddy is a good resource to a new co-worker; and the supervisor can provide career and development advice as a relationship grows.

Onboarding Planning Tool

Decide when each item is to be done by using these codes:

P = prior to first day
FD = first day
FW = first week
FM = first month
SM = second month
Decide *who* takes care of each item by using these codes:
HR = Human Resources
S = new employee's supervisor
E = employee – self directed
B = new employee's assigned "buddy" or co-worker

Organization
Who When

_____ _____ History/Mission/Vision/Organizational philosophy & objectives

_____ _____ Organizational structure

_____ _____ Products and services

_____ _____ Customers

_____ _____ Employee's department

_____ _____ How departments relate to employee's department

_____ _____ Plant Tour & facility layout with map

_____ _____ Union representation referral

Compensation
Who When

_____ _____ Pay schedule

_____ _____ Timecard

_____ _____ Overtime

_____ _____ Payroll deductions

_____ _____ Direct deposit options

_____ _____ Employee Records

_____ _____ Charities

_____ _____ Workers' compensation

_____ _____ Salary reviews

Benefits
Who When

_____ _____ Medical plan

_____ _____ Dental plan

_____ _____ Life insurance

_____ _____ Pension plan

_____ _____ Credit union

_____ _____ Savings plan

_____ _____ Incentive programs

_____ _____ Service and recognition awards

_____ _____ Employee purchases

_____ _____ Profit sharing plan

Professional development
Who When

_____ _____ Tuition reimbursement

_____ _____ Training and development programs

_____ _____ Buddy program

Attendance
Who When

_____ _____ Work hours

_____ _____ Rules about lateness, sickness, absence

Leave and holidays
Who When

_____ _____ Holidays

_____ _____ Leave policy

_____ _____ Family Medical Leave

_____ _____ Vacation

_____ _____ Jury duty

Health and safety
Who When

_____ _____ Safety
_____ _____ Emergency procedure
_____ _____ Evacuation routes and fire drills
_____ _____ HACCP
_____ _____ First aid
_____ _____ What to do in case of an accident
_____ _____ Driving company equipment
_____ _____ Child-care program
_____ _____ Wellness program
_____ _____ Employee-assistance program
_____ _____ Drug-free workplace

Security
Who When

_____ _____ Security procedures
_____ _____ Restricted areas
_____ _____ Name badge
_____ _____ Confidentiality and non-competition statement
_____ _____ Loyalty oath
_____ _____ Drug testing

Internal communications
Who When

_____ _____ Organization newsletter
_____ _____ Organization bulletin board
_____ _____ Employee handbook
_____ _____ Voice-mail operation
_____ _____ Standards for outgoing voice-mail messages

Transportation
Who When

_____ _____ Carpooling/ride sharing
_____ _____ Parking
_____ _____ Public transportation available
_____ _____ Permits, restricted areas

Personal comfort
Who When

_____ _____ Rest and meal breaks

_____ _____ Meet teammates

_____ _____ Cafeteria/break facilities

_____ _____ Recycling programs

_____ _____ Smoking policy

_____ _____ Rest-room locations

_____ _____ Safeguarding personal belongings/lockers

_____ _____ Lunch the first day

_____ _____ Sports activities

_____ _____ Recreational facilities and programs

Performance
Who When

_____ _____ What is expected of employees –Job Description/
Job Standards

_____ _____ Food handling

_____ _____ Ethical standards

_____ _____ Conflict of interest

_____ _____ Probationary period

_____ _____ Dress code - Whites/No exposed jewellery

_____ _____ Probationary Period

_____ _____ Promotions

_____ _____ Performance reviews

_____ _____ Disciplinary process

_____ _____ Causes for termination

_____ _____ Personal calls and visitors

_____ _____ Suggestions

_____ _____ Sexual harassment

_____ _____ Who to go to if you have a problem

7 Steps to Setting Up a Buddy System

1. Determine what the role of a buddy is:
_____ Provide information for the new employee on policies, procedures, work rules, norms

_____ Help the new employee clarify assignments

_____ Help socialize the new employee

_____ Assist in training the new employee

_____ Be a lunch companion

_____ Be a tour guide

_____ Provide feedback and encouragement to the new employee

_____ Identify resources

_____ Help, temporarily, to sort priorities for the new employee

_____ Provide introductions

2. Determine who will be a buddy. The most effective choice for a "buddy":
_____ Has been employed more than one year

_____ Is compatible with the new employee (age, education, temperament, culture, language)

_____ Is given time to be accessible to the new employee

_____ Has a good performance history

_____ Is skilled in the new employee's job

_____ Is proud of the organization

_____ Is a peer of the new employee

_____ Has patience and good communication and interpersonal skills

_____ Wants to be a "buddy"

_____ Is a positive role model (well-regarded and accepted by current employees)

_____ Has been selected in advance and trained in "buddy" role.*

3. Determine time line and time commitment required to train the buddy on their role and allow for adequate time for the buddy to assist in the new employee's on-boarding.

4. **Train the buddy so they** understand their role and responsibilities. For example, do they have copies of all your training documentation? Do they understand the kind of support that they are being asked to provide?

5. **Monitor the relationship**. Once buddies are matched with new employees, it is important to keep in touch with both parties to make sure that the relationship is working out. You don't need to sit down every week with both people, but you might implement an "open door" policy where either party can contact you if they are having problems. Alternatively, you might review the relationship and how it is working after the first two weeks.

6. **Implement ongoing improvement**. It is important that there is an ongoing evaluation for buddy systems to ensure that the system itself is working. A simple exit survey can be used to evaluate the effectiveness of the buddies you are using and the structures you have in place to support the program. Give the new employee a chance to give you some feedback – this empowers the new employee to contribute to possible improvements in the system.

7. **Recognize the buddy's efforts**. Buddies bring tremendous value to the employee on-boarding process and should be recognized for their efforts in some meaningful way. Some food processors pay extra to their buddies, others acknowledge their contributions with gift certificates or other low-cost yet highly appreciated examples of recognition.

Onboarding Effectiveness Survey - Evaluation by New Employee

Please read the following statements & *circle the number that describes how you feel:*

During your first few days with the company how often did you feel:

	Never	Never Almost	Fairly Often	Always
Welcome	0	1	2	3
Safe	0	1	2	3
Important	0	1	2	3
Proud	0	1	2	3
Happy	0	1	2	3
Confident	0	1	2	3
Respected	0	1	2	3
Confused	0	1	2	3
Frustrated	0	1	2	3
Worried	0	1	2	3
Bored	0	1	2	3
Nervous	0	1	2	3
Afraid	0	1	2	3
Upset	0	1	2	3

	Strongly Disagree	Disagree	Agree	Strongly Agree
I know what is expected of me	0	1	2	3
It was easy to get answers to my questions	0	1	2	3
I had enough training to do my job	0	1	2	3
I received all the things that I needed to do my job	0	1	2	3
The people involved in my orientation were helpful	0	1	2	3
The paper work was easy to understand	0	1	2	3
My supervisor cares about me as a person	0	1	2	3
My co-workers care about me as a person	0	1	2	3
I know how well I am doing at my job	0	1	2	3
The job is what I expected when I was hired	0	1	2	3
I am satisfied with my job	0	1	2	3
I am happy that I am working with this company	0	1	2	3

1. What were the most helpful items covered during orientation?
2. What items were not helpful, not needed, or could have waited until later to be addressed?
3. What items were not covered during the initial meeting that you want to know about?
4. What questions do you have about information presented that did not occur to you at the time of the first meeting?
5. Are there issues you want to discuss in confidence with a Human Resources representative?
6. Have you discussed these confidential matters with your supervisor?
7. Did you have enough guidance to complete the self-directed portion of the orientation?
8. How can the "buddy" program be improved?

Post-Orientation Evaluation by Supervisor

It has been two months since your new employee, *[name]*
_____, attended his or her initial orientation event. A great deal of information was offered and presented concerning our policies, procedures, and benefits. Your perspective on the information that was given is important. Please answer these questions to help complete the first phase of your new employee's on-boarding and to assist us in improving our orientation program.

1. What information has the employee asked about that could have been included in the initial meeting?
2. What items at the initial presentation were not helpful, not needed, or could have waited until later to be addressed?
3. What further information does the employee need?
4. What skill training does the employee need?
5. What issues about the new employee do you want to discuss in confidence with a Human Resources representative?
6. What follow-up by the Human Resources department does the new employee need in the next three months?
7. What additional guidance did this employee need in order to complete the self-directed portion of orientation?
8. How can the "buddy" program be improved?

3. Interpersonal relations and communications experience

The most important aspect of maintaining superior human relations is the leaders' ability to communicate with their team. Food for thought: "All good leaders are great listeners." Effective leaders need to be aware of the seven most common barriers to communication:

1. Uncommon symbols or slang. Sometimes we have a tendency to overuse industry jargon. Do not assume that everyone understands what you are talking about.
2. Lack of communications training.
3. Environmental disturbances—excessive background noise or message overload.
4. Improper attitude, assumptions or personal biases.
5. Cultural, educational, or age differences between sender and receiver.
6. The sender/receiver relationship.
7. Speed of thought—the average adult processes words into sentences at approximately 500 words per minute, but can only speak 150 words per minute. The challenge is to stay focused on the meaning of the words and to discipline your mind from wandering. Another powerful and quick reminder for winning human relations is what I call the rule of 70/30. This rule reminds us that when we are communicating with others we should limit our speaking to 30 percent of the conversation, thus we can listen 70 percent of the time. This is important because it is impossible to learn if we are not listening.

There are three ways to improve overall effectiveness of communications:

1. Clarity—say exactly what you mean
2. Honesty—say how you feel
3. Directness—say what you want

Note: *As the leader you are 100 percent responsible for both sending and receiving the communication.*

A few years ago I saw the following done up as a poster, I think that it is self-explanatory.

A Short Course in Human Relations

The 6 most important words:
I admit I made a mistake
The 5 most important words:
You did a good job
The 4 most important words:
What is your opinion?
The 3 most important words:
If you please
The 2 most important words:
Thank you
The most important word:
We
The least important word:

4. Training & development experience

It may seem obvious, but the fact remains that training your employees is one of the best business investments you can make. By investing in the development of your people not only do you improve productivity, client satisfaction, and profits, but you also communicate a strong message that you value your employees and you expect that they will be with you in the future. An interesting perspective with younger workers contrary to the commonly held notion by many baby boomer bosses, that generation X's and Y's will stick around with the same employer if the working conditions encourage them to do so. One of the biggest retention strategies to hang on to your younger talent is to continuously invest in them through formal training and development and with ongoing coaching and mentoring, coupled with interesting and challenging projects to learn from. A big part of the self identity of these younger workers is the desire to continue to get meaningful learning experiences while adding to the depth of their resumes. It's ironic that the more opportunities they see to improve their marketability with your company the less likely that they will leave.

Training needs assessment and action plan

One of the greatest on-the-job "productivity robbers" is the gap between what the job requires and what the employee is actually able to do. This tool helps the supervisor to quickly and accurately assess the training needs of each employee by identifying their skills or knowledge gaps. It also helps prioritize the training and determine the necessary budget to ensure the employee quickly becomes more productive.

Training needs assessment and planner

Employee Name: _____

Job Title: _____

Length of time on the job: _____

Steps in identifying training needs (to be done by both the supervisor and the employee):

1. Review the job description focusing on key tasks of the job.
2. Determine the skills and knowledge required to perform each task.
3. Identify any skill or knowledge "gaps" that the employee requires training in.

Key Job Tasks	Skills/Knowledge Required	Identified Skills/ Knowledge Gap

Type of Training Required to fill skills/knowledge gap	Training	Budget	Priority; High, medium, low	Date for Training completion
New employee orientation				
Safety Course				
On-the-job				
Job Shadowing/ Buddy System				
More experienced co-worker shows new employee the "ropes"				
Apprentice Training				
Job Rotation/ Cross Training				
Employee gets to experience other jobs within workplace				
Coaching/ Mentoring				
Supervisor takes employee "under their wing" teaches and guides them in their development				
Self-directed Study				
(Books, CDs, DVDs)				
External Workshop				
External Seminar/Conference				
On-line Course				
Training learned via the internet				
Continuing Education				
Offered through high schools, community colleges and municipal recreation departments.				
College/ University				

Maximize ROI on Training

This tool illustrates every major step of the training process (before, during and after) including the key people who should be involved in the process. The point of this tool is to ensure that you get the highest possible return on your training investments.

Process to maximize your training return on investment	When this should happen			Who should be involved		
	Before Training	During Training	After Training	Trainer	Boss	Trainee
Involve boss, and trainee in identifying need for training	X				X	X
Identify specific job related skill gaps that training will fill in.	X				X	X
Ensure that training budget is identified and approved	X			X	X	
Identify best training method to fill skills gap	X			X	X	
Obtain trainee "buy-in" to being on training	X				X	X
Provide training in a positive learning environment		X		X	X	X
Test trainee for understanding		X		X	X	X
Provide trainee opportunity to practice new skills		X		X	X	X
Provide trainee feedback on training and new skills development		X		X	X	
Recognize trainee's progress, both positives and negatives		X		X	X	
Seek trainees feedback on training, both positive and negative			X	X	X	X
Seek boss' feedback on impact of training on trainee's performance			X		X	
Re-enforce trainee's new skills over time so bad habits don't emerge			X		X	X
Modify/ improve training if needed			X	X		

5. Receiving informal feedback and formal performance evaluation experience

Providing valuable performance feedback

People crave feedback. In fact, even during leisure and recreation activities they want to know "the score". The key thing to remember is to provide valuable performance feedback in a timely, constructive and positive manner. The employer needs to provide the employee with feedback to enhance performance and increase the level of productivity.

A leader's approach to assessing their staff's on-the-job performance and how they provide feedback on that performance has direct link to employee productivity, job satisfaction, and reduction of errors and wastage which impacts your profits. Employees who know what is expected of them on the job, and see that there is a performance feedback process and that it is fair and effective will be more committed to the company.

Self-check: Assessing others on-the-job performance

Read each statement and score on a scale of 1 being totally not accurate and 10 being very accurate. The higher the number, the more the statement reflects you. Then add up the total of all of your scores.

Statements	Score
I let the employee do most of the talking.	
I make an effort to listen to the employee's ideas.	
I am prepared to suggest solutions to the employee.	
My evaluation comments are performance based.	
I focus and re-enforce the positive.	
I try to support and encourage the employee's ideas.	
I invite alternatives & do not assume there is only one path.	
I use open-ended questions to stimulate discussion.	
I am specific when I'm concerned about performance.	
My employees know I want them to succeed.	
I like being responsible for leading team productivity.	
I like people and enjoy talking with them.	
I don't mind giving constructive criticism.	
I provide praise freely and often when earned.	
Workers who tell me what they think don't intimidate me.	
I seek and use new ideas whenever possible.	
I respect the skills & knowledge of my employees.	
I follow up on commitments & goals that were set.	
I am sensitive to the needs and feelings of others.	
I'm not worried if employees know more than I do.	
Total	

Interpretation:

A score between 180 and 200 indicates you should be very successful in conducting performance appraisals. Scores between 140 and 179 indicate significant strength plus a few improvements needed. A score between 100 and 139 reflects some strength, but a significant number of problem areas as well. Scores below 100 call for a serious effort to improve in several categories. Make a special effort to grow in any area where you scored 6 or less regardless of your total score.

Performance Evaluation Checklist

This tool is a simple checklist designed to help the supervisor in the preparation, conducting and follow through of employee performance discussions.

The following checklist is designed to guide the supervisor in preparing, conducting and following through on employee performance appraisal discussions.

Before the meeting:
- Choose a time and place to hold meeting that will minimize work disruption for supervisor and employee
- Tell the employee well in advance of the meeting and explain the process
- Give employee enough time to prepare
- Allocate sufficient time for a two-way open discussion
- Gather all necessary examples and documents relating to performance

During the meeting:
- Provide employee with questions to be discussed at the meeting
- Always start and end on a positive note
- Focus on employee's performance and behaviours not their personality
- Use real examples of behaviours you have observed when providing feedback
- Don't allow interruptions during meeting
- Always encourage employee to provide their point of view on the issue being discussed
- Don't gloss over or make excuses for problems
- Encourage employee to suggest ways to improve
- Be positive and supportive when providing constructive criticism
- Set a time to follow up discussion in the future

Performance Evaluation Template

This ready-to-use tool is a fill-in-the blank form designed to be completed separately by the supervisor and employee prior to their discussion. This allows both parties to contribute constructively to the discussion.

Performance Evaluation Template

Employee Name:	Position:	Review Date:
Date last Review:	Length of time in position:	

Explanation of Ratings

"E" = Excellent – Individual performs all tasks in an exceptional manner. Requires little supervision.

"G" = Good – Individual performs most tasks well. Requires occasional supervision.

"S" = Satisfactory – Individual performs most tasks satisfactorily. Requires normal supervision.

"F" = Fair – Individual performs some tasks satisfactorily, but not all. Requires more than normal supervision.

"U" = Unsatisfactory – Individual fails to perform many tasks satisfactorily.
Requires close and constant supervision.

"Mistakes are part of the dues one pays for a full life."

Sophia Loren

Rating Factors	U	F	S	G	E	Comments
Job Understanding: Employee possesses a clear knowledge of the responsibilities and the task they must perform.						
Job Performance: The neatness, thoroughness and accuracy of employee's work.						
Job Productivity: The quality of the employee's work in terms of volume and accomplishments.						
Dependability: The reliability of this employee in terms of being on time and completion of tasks, targets or goals?						
Cooperation: The employee's willingness to work well with teammates.						
Overall Rating						

Comments on how past objectives were met.

Specific comments as to employee's strengths and accomplishments.

Specific comments as to employee's areas for improvement.

Specific future goals/ objectives agreed upon.

Other comments of the employee.

Employee Signature:	**Date:**
Supervisor Signature:	**Date:**
Witness Signature:	**Date:**
Date next Review:	**Length of time in position:**

Talking through performance problems

This tool guides the supervisor through a "conservational approach" to resolve performance problems with their employee.

Questions (If "Yes" Response move on to next question below)	If "No" Response
1. Is employee aware of their job duties?	Tell employee what to do
2. Is employee aware of their performance?	Arrange for performance feedback
3. Is employee aware of performance standards?	Explain performance standards
4. Does employee see a need to improve?	Explain impact their performance has on company success and obtain commitment for future improvement.
5. Does employee have necessary skills & knowledge to do the job as expected?	Provide needed training and development
Questions (If "No" Response move on to next question below)	**If "Yes" Response**
6. Does the job appear to be too complex or big for the employee?	Consider reassignment, dividing some of the duties or provide additional training
7. Does employee lack tools, equipment, materials, funds, support staff or other resources?	Provide needed resources
8. Is the employee's poor work being rewarded?	Eliminate the inappropriate rein forces and only reward positive behaviours
9. Is the employee's good work being punished or is there peer pressure against good work?	Eliminate the source of punishment and reinforce the positive behaviours
10. Is the employee apathetic, negative or unconcerned? Increase employee's level of motivation and commitment by coaching them. .	If this does not work use positive discipline

If you have been through the first 10 steps without satisfaction, the final step is to restate your performance expectations and provide the opportunity for the employee to improve. If you are still not getting the desired results then both parties should "face the facts" that this might not be the best fit for the employee and they should be encouraged to seek more suitable employment opportunities elsewhere.

6. Employee level of satisfaction experience

Obviously, everyone wants happy, satisfied and productive workers. One of the easiest ways to gauge the satisfaction of the entire team is to invite them to fill out and submit this tool. It will give very valuable insights on specific areas that can positively impact moral. The key to success with all surveys is to make sure that your people don't fear them. If they are suspicious of your intentions they won't likely share openly in writing. The easiest way to overcome this is to keep the surveys confidential by not having people identify themselves on the survey and by handing them in a blank envelop or dropping them in a "ballot" type box. As with all staff surveys, you only get partial value by receiving the comments from staff, but you fully capitalize on the tool when you invite staff to brainstorm creative ideas to resolve any identified challenges.

Staff Satisfaction Survey

The following survey is a sample of a staff satisfaction survey that you can provide to all employees:

The following survey is an opportunity for you to provide feedback on your level of satisfaction while working at the company. We strive to make our company a place where every team mate will be both happy and productive and we greatly appreciate your feedback as we continue to improve. The completion of the survey is both voluntary and confidential. It is offered to all employees to take a few moments to fill it out, fold it and place it in the envelope provided and drop it in the cardboard box marked "Survey" on the supervisor's desk.

Directions: *Read each statement and score on a scale of 1 being totally not accurate and 10 being very accurate. The higher the number, the more the statement reflects how you view the situation.*

Statement	Score
Training and Development	
I am provided with opportunities to improve my skills with this company.	
I am satisfied with the training I receive on the job.	
I am satisfied with the opportunity for job advancement with this company.	
I am happy with how my career is progressing with this company.	
Work Group	
Most days things run smoothly at work.	
I get along well with my team mates.	
We enjoy positive team morale.	
Work is evenly distributed among the team.	
Working Conditions	
Personal health and safety takes priority over production.	
I have the necessary tools/ resources to do the job well.	
Work Performance	
I feel that workload, performance expectations placed on me are reasonable.	
It is easy to get needed job related information.	
I feel supported by my team mates to assist me in doing my job well.	
Supervisory Support	
I feel supported by my supervisor to assist me in doing my job well.	
I trust my supervisor.	
My supervisor is honest and open with me.	
My supervisor listens to my suggestions and or concerns.	
My supervisor makes it clear what they expect of me.	
My supervisor provides useful feedback on my performance.	
My supervisor treats me fairly.	
My supervisor treats me with respect as an individual.	
My supervisor keeps me informed of upcoming changes that affect my job.	
My supervisor leads by example of what is acceptable workplace behaviour.	

7. The boss experience

The "boss" is a key element in reducing employee turnover, increasing staff satisfaction and levels of productivity. Everyone who supervises one or more people is a leader, and as a leader you set the tone for the overall work environment. In short, you are the "model" of communications and performance standards to your entire team.

Leadership Effectiveness Self-Check

The following tool is a quick "self-check" that covers most of the key mindsets of effective leaders. It provides a quick snapshot of your strengths and opportunities to enhance your leadership effectiveness. The stronger the leader, the stronger the team. To best take advantage of this tool every supervisor should fill this out and then discuss with their boss. The business owner could discuss with their business partner, spouse or another business owner. The purpose of these discussions is to focus on areas of personal development.

Directions: Read each statement and score on a scale of 1 being totally inaccurate and 10 being very accurate. The higher the number, the more the statement reflects you. Then add up the total of all of your scores.

Statements	Score
I promote teamwork and discourage "us versus them" thinking.	
I provide clear directions on how the job should be done.	
I set the example of how my team should work together.	
I create an environment where people feel respected, valued and appreciated.	
I encourage the giving & receiving of feedback.	
I help employees focus on key activities that contribute to our company success.	
I create an environment focused on productivity.	
I clearly communicate the company goals so everyone can contribute to them.	
I set clear expectations & let people know how well they are meeting them.	
I set high standards for my performance and I encourage others to do the same.	
I involve my people in making decisions.	
I encourage and reward creativity and innovation.	
I encourage people to stretch beyond their current abilities.	
I praise people publicly and I criticise privately.	
I model enthusiasm & loyalty to the company and the brand.	
I help people take ownership of results by holding them accountable.	
Total	

Interpretation:

A score between 140 and 160 indicates you should be a very successful leader. Scores between 120 and 140 indicate significant strength plus a few improvements needs. A score between 90 and 120 reflects some strength, but a significant number of problem areas as well. Scores below 90 call for a serious effort to improve in several categories. Make a special effort to grow in any area where you scored 6 or less regardless of your total score.

8. Employee recognition experience

Look up the words *recognize* or *recognition* in any dictionary and you will find definitions that use words such as "see", "identify", and "acknowledge". These words are at the core of what effective employee recognition is about. Employee recognition means management cares enough to take the time to see, identify and acknowledge the organizational contributions, valued behaviours and good efforts of employees. Recognition is an essential element to any successful working relationship. Employees must know that their work matters and is important to the company.

As individuals, not all people value the same recognition for similar activities or behaviours. Personalizing the recognition process is the most effective way to motivate and increase performance, develop employee skill, acknowledge, contributions, and meet organizational objectives.

Benefits of Employee Recognition -the Link between Recognition and Performance

There are a number of recognition-performance links that directly impact employers in the following ways:

- Recognizing employees helps management motivate staff.
- Providing recognition to line workers when they do good work increases performance.
- Recognizing employees provides them with practical feedback.
- Recognizing employees for good work makes it easier to get the work done.
- Providing recognition helps achieve corporate goals.
- Providing recognition helps achieve job specific goals.

12 Benefits of Employee Recognition for Employers

- Motivates employees by acknowledging their achievements.
- Enhances individual's self-worth and self-confidence.
- Reinforces positive behaviours to both individual and entire team.
- Positive workplace draws passive job seekers & increases likelihood of employee referrals.
- Reduces employee turnover & absenteeism.

- Fosters a sense of pride in work and company.
- Enhances relationship between supervisors and workers.
- Promotes positive open communications.
- Creates loyal employees.
- Improves productivity.
- Reinforces company culture and values & aligns desired behaviours with company goals.
- Increases profits.

Building an Employee Recognition Program

While there is more than one way to design an effective employee recognition program, many successful programs share common attributes. The most effective recognition programs typically use a systems approach to develop a "culture of recognition." They reflect the organization's values and business strategy. They are clearly defined and well-publicized. They involve employees in program design and implementation, and are multi-layered (organization-wide and unit-specific). While maintaining creativity and fun they can still have a mix of formal and informal programs. To avoid stagnation, programs need to change periodically.

Building a timely and specific recognition program is more meaningful when supported with educational tools and when the reward is personalized to the individual.

The characteristics of effective recognition are:
- **Timely** – as soon as possible after the positive achievement
- **Proportional** – matches the action in type and degree of recognition
- **Specific** – identifies the positive behaviour
- **Individual** – recognizes the person involved in the action
- **Sincere** – comes from the heart and shows you care
- **Personal** – reflects the personality of the recipient

Three Keys to Effective Employee Recognition

1. Invest Time

To engage employees, consider making time for personal talk such as going for coffee together periodically or making time to inquire about their life outside of work. When you make time to show interest in a fellow employee, you are demonstrating recognition for the individual. Employees are more likely to share their interests, challenges and successes, if they feel that you are genuinely interested in what they have to say. Showing interest and engaging employees will be a minimal cost, yet effective way to begin a relationship, and to provide meaningful individual recognition.

2. Determine what is Important

Know what is important to employees, at work and outside of work. Recognition encompasses accepting each other as unique individuals and acknowledging that each of us has a life outside of work. This will enable a better understanding of employees, their values, and how you can demonstrate recognition effectively on an individual basis. In order to make recognition a valuable and meaningful tool, it is essential to determine what is important or perceived as valuable from an individual perspective.

3. Individualize

Finally, break into the core of recognition. Find out specifically when, what and how employees like to be recognized. Having employees who feel valued is an essential step to creating a healthy and positive workplace and enhancing performance. Employees who feel valued are likely to have increased performance, decreased absenteeism and turnover rates, and may be able to influence the morale of other employees in a healthy and positive way. When providing recognition at a personal level - keep it simple! Keep it spontaneous yet sincere. Start to take notes and comment on the things that are valued by that individual.

Three Approaches to Recognition

Day-to-Day - An ongoing no-cost approach given to anyone at anytime. The most powerful motivator is immediate recognition. Example: praise, thanks…

Informal - Includes low-cost, tangible gestures of appreciation. Example: certificates of appreciation, Starbucks or Tim Horton's gift cards…

Formal higher profile organization - wide events where all employees can receive recognition. Example: Long Service Awards, Company President's Award of Excellence…

Essential Elements of Recognition
- Match the recognition to the person according to what is important to them.
- Directly link recognition to performance and goal achievement.
- Be timely by giving recognition as soon as possible after desired behaviour.
- Always state why recognition is given to ensure clarity and repeat behaviour.
- Make it fair by allowing all employees equal opportunities for recognition.
- Be creative by using a variety of methods to recognize employees' accomplishments.
- Involve your team in determining what recognition they value.
- Give ongoing words of praise according to accomplishment.
- Always remember the golden words "Thank You".

Developing a rewards and recognition culture

Motivation does not have to cost a lot of money. All it takes is a bit of creativity and innovation tailored to the needs of your staff. This tool is in two parts: the first is a quick self-check to see how well you are developing a rewards and recognition culture within your company and the second part provides low cost/ high impact methods to reward your people.

Developing a rewards and recognition culture

One of the best ways to keep your people productive and happy is to develop a rewards and recognition culture. Below is a quick self-check to see how well you are doing. This section contains three surveys that will provide a quick snapshot as to your organizations overall rewards and recognition culture.

Directions: *Read each question and answer on the following scale; never, occasionally or regularly.*

Do you...	Never	Occasionally	Regularly
Find that the rewards are valued by staff?			
Differentiate between top and average performers?			
Match rewards with specific needs of employers?			
Reward top performers with new opportunities?			
Recognize small improvements in poor performers?			
Reward behaviour that supports company goals?			
Offer rewards based on measurable results?			
Seek input on what rewards would motivate employee?			
Communicate what is needed in order to earn rewards?			
Help employees overcome obstacles to success?			
Create a friendly competitive atmosphere among staff?			
Recognize both positive behaviours and results?			
Reward people in a way that they, not you value?			
Say thank you for routine work & small improvements?			
Say thank you to your boss and peers?			
Offer specific examples when praising an employee?			
Enrich employee's job to make them more interesting?			
Reward team members equally for team results?			
Reward solving problems rather than hiding them?			
Assist employee achieve work/life balance?			

By doing all of the following activities on a regular basis you will be on the fast-track to developing a rewards and recognition culture.

Seven simple steps to rewarding and recognizing employees:

1. Consider how you might like to be thanked for your efforts.
2. Ask them what type of reward would be appreciated by them.
3. Praise publicly and criticize privately.
4. Develop the habit of looking for reasons to praise people, it will raise the bar.
5. Identify the specific positive behaviour or performance being acknowledged.
6. Reward/ recognize positive performance as soon as possible to re-enforce behaviour.
7. Make the process fun and engaging.

List of low cost/high impact reward and recognition ideas worth considering:

- Sincere personal thank you or well done (verbally or in writing)
- Coffee shop gift certificates for immediate recognition
- Plush bull dog animal for most persistent employee
- Spark plug award for brightest idea
- Employee of the month
- Preferred parking spot for a week
- Gifts (T-shirt, ball caps, sweatshirts, mouse pads…)
- Gift certificate for night out at the movies for two
- Gift certificate for dinner for two
- Ice cream cake with "Awesome Job" on it
- Team BBQ
- Pre paid cell card
- Plaque
- Gift basket
- Digital camera
- Music CD or free I-Tunes downloads
- Gift certificate for spa
- Ticket to sport event
- Contribution to employee's charity of choice
- Paid day off

The following survey informs you how important your people rate various methods of motivation.

Survey of Staff Key Motivators

Please read the sentences below & circle the number that tells us how important these things are to you:

	Not	Sort of	Quite	Very
Being thanked by your supervisor	0	1	2	3
Praise in front of the people you work with	0	1	2	3
A certificate that proves you have done a good job	0	1	2	3
Getting thanked for your attendance at work	0	1	2	3
A thank you letter from the company	0	1	2	3
Getting a company award	0	1	2	3
Being thanked in the company newsletter	0	1	2	3
Getting cash for doing a good job	0	1	2	3
A gift card to buy something when you do a good job	0	1	2	3
Getting tickets to go to a special event	0	1	2	3
Getting a "years-of-service" award	0	1	2	3
Being named employee-of-the-month	0	1	2	3

The following survey informs you how often you provide various methods of motivation as rated by your people.

Survey of How Well We Motivate

Please read the sentences below & circle the number that tells how often these things HAPPEN for you:

	Never	Sometimes	Often
Being thanked by your supervisor	0	1	2
Being told you do a good job in front of the people you work with	0	1	2
Getting a certificate that proves you have done a good job	0	1	2
Getting thanked for my attendance at work	0	1	2
A letter from the company thanking you for doing a good job	0	1	2
Getting a company award	0	1	2
Being thanked in the company newsletter	0	1	2
Getting cash for doing a good job	0	1	2
A pre-paid card to buy something when you did a good job	0	1	2
Getting tickets to go to a special event	0	1	2
Getting a "years-of-service" award	0	1	2
Being named employee-of-the-month	0	1	2

9. Employee referral experience

An employee referral occurs when an existing employee encourages someone they know to apply to work for the same company or when the employee notifies their employer about a potential future employee that is part of their social network. By encouraging your good workers to invite their friends and family to apply to work at your company you are turning your entire team into recruiters that can sell your company—and its available positions—to some potentially great candidates.

Benefits of Establishing an Employee Referral Program

Employees can be your best recruiters. By implementing a well thought out employee referral program, your company will enjoy many significant benefits. Research has shown that employees hired through referrals typically display the following positive qualities over their non-referral counterparts:

- Less cost to "reach", resulting in reduced advertising and search firm fees
- Less time to recruit
- Have greater understanding of what the job entails
- Adapt more quickly to new job and company culture
- Display higher levels of performance sooner
- Fit-in quicker with existing team
- Stay with companies for longer periods of time

Building an Employee Referral Program

There is no one right way to build a referral program – every company is different. An important fact to keep in mind is that each referral program you run has a shelf life. To keep your employees interested you need to change the theme of your program every 6 months or so. As was mentioned before, the most important factor in determining the success of an employee referral program is the "referrability" of the company. The following are a few additional things you should consider doing to ensure that your referral program will be a success.

Get employee buy-in

The first step to building a program is to get your employees, from management to line workers on board, as they will become your source for new hires. This is called getting a buy-in. Your employees need to believe in the referral program to become involved in it. A successful referral program starts at the top with continual reinforcement from the president/ general manager or plant manager. If you can't get your management team on board with the referral program your employees won't find value in it.

Promoting your referral program is one way to reinforce its importance and keep enthusiasm for the program alive. Continuously promote the referral program every chance you get; one on-one, or in weekly meetings. Showing that you are excited and active in the success of the program will help win over the rest of your company. Track and publicize all the numbers related to your program for all to see.

Determine the reward

The rewards will be different depending on whom you are targeting for the referrals. If your reward is financial, be cautious. Sizeable cash rewards may result in an overwhelming number of unqualified candidates. If the reward is too small, or something your employees aren't interested in no one will pay attention. If you are committed to giving out a cash reward ask your employees what amount it would take to motivate them and base your reward on their answers. Money is a motivator but shouldn't be the only motivator considered as a reward for a successful referral.

Here are some non cash suggestions for rewards:

- Sports matches tickets
- Paid days off
- Gift card for popular store (Wal-Mart, CDN Tire etc)
- Certificate for dinner for two at local restaurant

Some people reward each employee individually for a referral that was hired while some put the names of all the employees that passed on excellent referrals into a hat for a draw. These rewards tend to be bigger, since only one reward is given out. Prizes can run the gamut from free airline tickets or a cruise vacation, to an extra paid week of vacation time. You can reward your employees however you see fit, but you need to be sure the reward is something your employees will respond to or the program simply won't work. After all, what might sound enticing to one person may sound foolish to another. Consider a cross promotion with a supplier or sister company, or perhaps a sponsor to provide a draw.

Be creative when promoting the program

When building a referral program think like a marketer. Find a fun and clever theme that grabs your employees' attention. The most important thing is the audience – know what they will respond to. Some people will respond to a cash reward while others will respond to gift cards or electronic gadgets. Find out what will drive your employees. One company recently used a clever theme to promote their referral program. It was called "Go Fish" and all around the cafeteria huge, colourful paper mache fish hung from the ceiling. Whenever an employee referred a useful candidate to the company they got a miniature version of the big fish and their name went into a fish bowl for a raffle at the end of the program.

Maintain the program with open communication

Open communication is key. If a referral program is not giving the results you had hoped, talk with your employees and managers to get to the root of the problem. Also, it is important to keep your employees in the loop when it comes to where their referrals stand so that their contributions are taken seriously. One way to do this is to guarantee an interview with anyone who was referred by an employee. You also must be honest with the referred candidates. If a referral isn't quite right for the position or company, they may know someone else who might be. A referral program is about building relationships – the more relationships you have the bigger the pool of candidates.

Assess the results

As with any business practice, a referral program must be reviewed regularly for effectiveness. The most common way to assess the success of a referral program is to look at the percentage of new hires that come from referrals, how well they work out, how long they stay with the company, how quickly vacancies can be filled and how the overall cost-to-hire is reduced.

You also should measure your referral promotions against each other to find out which ones garnered the best results. If something didn't work, learn from the experience.

Remember to change your referral program to keep it interesting and rewarding for your employees. By using different themes and rewards you will breathe life into your referral efforts.

Things to keep in mind
There are not too many pitfalls to having a referral program, but there are a few things to keep in mind to keep one running effectively:

- Life span of the program – No matter how wonderful your referral program is it still has a shelf life. To keep your employees motivated you need to change the theme or rewards of the bonus program to get their attention.
- Problems with the attribution of referral – It is a small world and having two employees refer the same great candidate does happen. Make sure to establish some ground rules and stipulations on referrals before promoting your program.
- Make the rules simple – Complex submission rules will dissuade employees from participating. Try to create guidelines that are easily understood. However, make sure you address problematic areas, such as how to deal with a situation in which two people claim to have referred the same candidate who ultimately was hired.
- Maintain clear records – By time-dating each resume that has a properly filled out referral card for example, you can avoid potential problems. Keep data that list the referral, the date, the name of the candidate, all pertinent candidate data, a copy of the resume/application, and a copy of the referral form. Also, when the status of the referral changes, update it accordingly.

Communicating Employee Referral Program

Use pay cheque stuffers and the company newsletter or intranet to publicize the program. Announce special events, such as giveaways or quarterly drawings, as well as the status of the overall program and the status of individuals referred. Consider sending out a direct mail piece to all of your employee's home addresses. This works on two levels. First, the advertisement is at home and it is easy to show friends and family. Secondly, if a spouse or family member learns that the employee is eligible to receive a nice bonus for referring someone, they will often encourage or remind the employee to submit the referral.

Sample Staff Referrals Program

Employee Name: _____ Employee # : _____

Name of Referred: _____ Contact Information: _____

To be completed by

Human Resources Position Hired For: _____ Date Hired: _____

Referral Incentive Time line: (Length of time worked by referred employee)

$ 100.00 - 480/hours worked Cheque # _____ Date issued/Direct deposit:_____

$ 100.00 - 960/hours worked Cheque # _____ Date issued/Direct deposit:_____

$ 100.00 - 1440/hours worked Cheque # _____ Date issued/Direct deposit: _____

Notes:
- It is the responsibility of the referring employee to notify Human Resources by completing the top portion of this form and submitting it directly to a Human Resources representative.
- The employee that made the referral will be notified if their referral was hired or not.
- Referral incentive cheques will be paid on the pay run following the new hires fulfilling each time line milestone.
- This program is open to all employees except human resources and senior management.
- Referral incentives are subject to income taxation.
- The referring employee must be currently employed with the company in order to receive payment.
- Employees are allowed to refer multiple people over the duration of the Employee Referral Program
- Referred employees must not have been employed with the company during the past 90 days in order to qualify for this program.

The following survey is a quick check to gage the overall effectiveness of your organization's staff referral program.

Survey- Review of Staff Referral Program

Please check one: I was hired:

❑ less than 6 months ago   ❑ more than 6 months ago

(Please check **one** response for each question)

	Yes	No
Did you know that the company has a program that gives you money if you get someone to work at the company?		
Do you know how the Employee Referral program works at the company?		
Do you feel that the company wants you to tell people to work at the company?		
Have you ever told someone to apply for a job with this company?		
If you have not told anyone to apply for a job with this company, why not?		
Is it easy to use the company's Employee Referral Program?		
If you did get someone to apply for a job at the company in the past, did you like the way that you were treated by the company for getting that person to apply?		
Do you feel that the company contacted the person that applied for the job fast enough?		
Did the company thank you for getting the person to apply for the job?		
Was the person that you got to apply for the job hired by the company?		
Is it easy to use the company's Employee Referral Program?		
If the person that you got to apply for the job was hired, are they still working with the company?		
If the person is no longer working for the company, why did they leave?		
In the future would you likely refer someone to work here?		

If you were the boss of the company, how would you get your employees to ask people to apply for jobs at your company?

_____

_____

_____

10. Employee exiting experience

Lessons Learned

It is unfortunate when good people leave an organization. There are many factors that can contribute to the employee's decision to leave. Some of which may be beyond the control of the employer, however it is in the best interest of the company to discover any issues that are within the company's control so they can resolve not to let history repeat itself and more employees are not lost in the future.

Employee Exit Interviews

The best way to understand what worked and what did not work from a recent employee quitting is to conduct an exit interview before they leave or shortly after. This tool makes it easy to gain valuable insights as to why an employee quits their job, and offers the opportunity to learn from the situation.

Employee Exit Interview

Attempt to have a "neutral" person (not the immediate supervisor) conduct the interview. The following two pages is a ready to use exit interview questionnaire.

Question	Agree	Disagree
I knew what was expected of me at work.		
I had the materials and equipment I needed to do my work right.		
I had the opportunity to do what I do best each day.		
My supervisor set an example for others to follow.		
I received recognition or praise for doing good work.		
My supervisor seemed to care about me as a person.		
My supervisor treated me with dignity and respect.		
My supervisor gave me useful feedback on my performance.		
My supervisor gave me timely feedback on my performance.		
My pay was inline with my level of education and experience.		
My benefits were an incentive to remain employed by the company.		
There was someone at work who encouraged my development.		
At work, my opinions seemed to count.		
The mission/purpose of my company made me feel my job was important.		
My fellow employees were committed to doing quality work.		
I had a best friend at work.		
In the last six months my supervisor talked to me about my progress.		
This last year, I had opportunities to learn and grow at work.		

The main reason(s) for leaving is/are:

_____ higher pay
_____ better benefits
_____ better chance for advancement
_____ my relationship with my supervisor
_____ the company work environment
_____ the lack of resources to adequately do my job
_____ other, please elaborate _____

What, if anything, could the organization have done that would have made it more likely for you to stay? _____

_____

_____

_____

_____

_____

_____

_____

_____

How referable is your organization?
Self Check – 10 Key Experiences

The following self check will get you started with an analysis of the work experience that your company delivers. Here is how to use it for maximum benefit:

1. Use the experiences as a starting point to generate a more complete checklist of experiences that defines the total employee experience.
2. Use the questions under each experience to analyze how you can improve the way you deliver that experience. As always, involve your senior leadership team and create an Employee Advisory Council comprised of a cross section of employees from the entire company in this process.
3. For each of the "10 Key Employee Experiences", ask the following:
    *   "What do our employees say they want from this interaction?"
    *   "The way we handle this… what emotions and perceptions does it leave with our employees?"
    *   "If we do it this new way, what emotions and perceptions would that leave with our employees?"
    *   "What emotions and perceptions do we want this moment of truth to create… and what do we need to do to create them?"
4. You can get the ball rolling by asking your employees "Do you have the kind of work experience at our company that makes you want to tell others that we're a great place to work? Does it make you want to recommend us to your friends and colleagues?"
5. Make sure you involve employees not only in data gathering, but in implementing changes. As in any change or organizational development initiative, the more you involve your employees in the process, the more invested they'll be, the better your data and the better the results.
6. Have your recruiters as well as your entire workforce share their positive experiences on-line via social networking. The remainder of this book will focus on how to capitalize on social media recruiting.

This final tool in Part 1 is meant to provide you with a quick analysis of how well your organization does in delivering on the 10 key employee experiences that has been the focus of the first half of the book.

1. Recruiting, Pre-selection, Job Offer and Welcoming Package Experience	Yes	No
Does your process leave applicants feeling respected?		
Does your process lead people to view your company as a well run outfit?		
Does your process lead people to view your company as an employer who cares about and respects its employees?		
Does the job offer clearly state the job being offered; start date and time, pay and benefits?		
Does the welcome package provide valuable information for the new recruit to review prior to the first day on the job?		
2. On-boarding- Pulling out the red carpet Experience	Yes	No
Is your orientation program inspiring?		
Does your orientation program leave new hires with the impression that you're a well run, professional outfit that does things right?		
Does your on-boarding process lead to new hires feeling that they are valued, that their employer cares about their well-being and success?		
3. Interpersonal Relations and Communications Experience	Yes	No
Do supervisors and manager listen to what employees have to say?		
Do employee concerns get addressed?		
If an employee concern doesn't result in change, is an explanation provided?		
Do managers respond with the same interest they would if their boss asked them?		
Are employee's ideas and input highly valued?		
Do employees receive the information and the "big picture" context that makes useful ideas possible?		
Are employees advised of the status of their ideas and if an idea isn't used, do they understand why?		
Are employees kept in the loop during change processes?		

4. Training & Development Experience		
Are individualized training need assessments conducted on each employee prior to engaging in training?		
Is a learning culture part of the organization?		
Does the company measure it's ROI on training & development efforts?		

5. Receiving Informal Feedback and Formal Performance Evaluation Experience	Yes	No
Do supervisors and managers provide regular feedback to employees?		
Do supervisors and managers know how to give feedback in clear, concrete terms?"		
Do supervisors and managers know how to give corrective feedback respectfully?		
Do supervisors and managers know how to invite employees to share their point of view so they feel understood?		
Do supervisors and managers integrate these conversations into a development plan?		
Are performance evaluations seen as a useful performance enhancement and professional development tool?		
Is the information contained in the performance evaluation truly a review of previous conversations?		
Are employees active participants in the review process, assessing their own performance?		
Is it safe for employees to disagree and not be perceived as disagreeable?		

6. Employee Level of Satisfaction Experience	Yes	No
Overall are the employees satisfied with their job?		
Overall are the employees satisfied with their employer?		
Overall are the employees satisfied with their boss?		
Overall are the employees satisfied with their co-workers?		

7. The Boss Experience	Yes	No
Is it safe for employees to voice their disagreements with their boss?		
Is honesty and openness valued, supported, and encouraged?		
Are managers coached about how to make it safe for employees to be open with them?		
Are managers held accountable for their behaviour toward employees?		

8. Employee Recognition Experience	Yes	No
Do employees feel appreciated?		
Do employees feel that going the extra mile is recognized and appreciated?		
Do employees feel that hard work and high performance is recognized by their boss and by		
9. Employee Referral Experience	**Yes**	**No**
Is the process involved in referring someone easy to do?		
Are employees aware of the employee referral program?		
Does the company quickly act upon the referral provided by contacting the referred person?		
Does the employee that provided the referral get acknowledged in some way?		
Are thanks given after referral?		
10. Employee Exiting Experience		
Was the real reason for the person's leaving identified?		
Was every reasonable effort made for both parties to part on positive terms?		
Were opportunities for internal improvements noted, communicated and implemented?		

Once you have mastered fulfilling these 10 key employee experiences, your company and your vacant positions will be referable. In other words your staff and all the people that they SERVICE will speak positively about your organization and your brand will grow both by positive reputation and by awareness. Part 2 of this book shows how to capitalize on all of your "employer of choice" efforts by tapping into the global talent pool through "word of mouth" via social media recruiting at the "speed of light"!

Part 2:
Capitalizing On Social Media Recruiting

To demonstrate the impact of social networking on our daily lives consider the experience of 21-year-old telecommunications student Andrew Meyer. It was noon, September 17, 2007 and US Senator John Kerry was speaking at the University of Florida in Gainesville. During Senator Kerry's speech Meyer's asked a question, was tasered and then forcibly removed from the venue. All this transpired very quickly. During the fray several students happened to catch the incident on their camera phones. The videos were posted on YouTube and the bloggers went on overdrive. Three hours later a local newspaper posted the video. It was the major play story on Fox News, ABC and CNN the following day with video replaying all day long. Within 48 hours of the event the video had 2.6 million views on YouTube and 2,000 blog posts. There were more than 7,000 blog posts within the week and 75% linked back to the YouTube video. The verb "tase" was added to the *New Oxford American Dictionary*, and was runner-up for word of the year, while Yale Book of Quotations designated "Don't Tase me, Bro!" the most memorable quote of 2007.

Don't Tase Me, Bro!

The reach of Social Media … and the numbers are growing daily!

LinkedIn
- 30 million users, strongly business-oriented, $1 Billion+ valuation
- Average age is 41
- 64% male, 36% female
- 95% of users have college degree

Facebook
- Australia recently allowed service of court documents via FB
- #5 top global website
- 132 million unique visitors/month
- Average age 24 (increasing .5 years every month)
- Fastest growth rate among those 35+ @ 39%/year

Twitter
- Has the fastest growth rate in social networking
- Is the network of choice for fortune 500's for marketing via social media
- Recently turned down $.5 Billion buyout offer from Facebook

YouTube
- Now the second leading search engine
- Bigger than Yahoo
- Accounts for 25% of all Google searches

MySpace
- Average age 35 (also increasing by .25 years/month)
- 68% of user base is 25+
- 41% of user base is 35-54!!!

These are just a sample of the most commonly known social networks sites to consider. There are so many others that are worth checking out. Wikipedia has a list of all major sites, their size and focus at, http://en.wikipedia.org/wiki/List_of_social_networking_websites

It's interesting to learn what work related activities people are doing when visiting social networks:

- 41% message a fellow student or colleague in the workplace
- 25% network with people sharing professional interests
- 17% blog about professional topics
- 10% collaborate on group projects
- 10% share suggestions to question's posted online
- 9% publish formal articles about professional topics
- 9% using polling features to get quick data

HR Tests the Social Networking Waters

According to Steve Williams, director of research at the Society for Human Resource Management, in mid 2008 just 3 percent of organizations used social networking as their primary recruitment source and about 17 percent used it as part of their hiring process. Of the organizations that used social media sites the most popular use of social networking was to source prospective candidates. 53 percent of respondents using social networking said they do so to search for passive candidates. Just over two-thirds say that social networking helps them reach candidates who they otherwise wouldn't know about or couldn't contact.

According to a recent CareerBuilder report, the number of companies using social networking web sites to screen potential employees has doubled in the last year, and what they have found has killed the hire for more than a third of candidates. In its survey of more than 2,600 hiring managers, CareerBuilder found that 45 percent are searching for information on job candidates on social networking sites. Facebook, LinkedIn and MySpace are the top sites being screened, but 11 percent of companies that are hiring are also searching blogs and 7 percent are following job applicants' Twitter postings.

So what is the attraction of social media recruiting that so many employers are jumping on the social networking wagon? Some of the advantages may include:

- They are free, or very in-expensive to use
- The size of their user base means that you can connect with many people

- People spend a lot of time on them so there can be frequent exposure to your brand
- Most believe what they read on them (credible)
- Less spam, so people use them in lieu of email
- They allow you to meet people that cannot be found on resume posting sites
- They are easy to learn and use
- They provide a global recruiting capability
- They can be used for prescreening
- Can be used in conjunction with blogs, podcasts, and the corporate website
- Social networks are now accessible from smart-phones (continuous access)
- You can use them to counter negative images
- Most individuals list their job title and where they work in their profiles
- Most people also provide valuable insights into their non-work interests
- They can add value during "slow" recruiting times
- Some allow you to easily add contacts by automatically searching your address book
- They can be fun

Be Aware of How You Use Online Information

Millions of potential job candidates have posted profiles on social media sites, and their number increases every minute. And as time goes by and careers advance, the online dossier of a given worker tends to get thicker with professional accomplishments or personal factoids, whether the individual purposely builds his/her presence on Facebook, LinkedIn, Twitter or another site, or the data on him/her accumulates passively. Once you tap into the power of Hired 2.0 you will start to amass candidates for your hiring pool, it's tempting to use Google and several other major social media sites to see what comes up. But the mix of public, private, professional and personal information that can be found online must be used with discretion.

> "Legal departments caution hiring managers that if they use social networking sites, they must verify the information to avoid liability. Misuse can lead to infringement of privacy or unintentional discrimination. If, for example, one allows information gleaned online about an applicant's age or marital status to affect a hiring decision, you could invite a lawsuit.
>
> "Companies must be very cautious when determining (a) if information acquired from the Internet is relevant to job performance and (b) where there is a legitimate, and legal reason to discount a candidate based on what they might have posted online," states Robert Capwell of Employment Background Investigations Inc. in his recent article for SHRM.
>
> **Source: Society for Human Resource Management**

Pre-screening using social media sites

Using Internet search engines such as Google, and social media sites to check out the background of applicants is becoming commonplace, "There's not a candidate I present whose name isn't 'Googled' by any organization that considers hiring them or even interviewing them," says Ivan H. Adler of the McCormick Group, an executive search consulting firm in Arlington, Va. "It's the very first thing."

Another reason to conduct online research on a candidate is to make sure you have accurate information. Given recent scandals involving prominent executives who falsified their credentials and a heightened emphasis on workplace security in general, people are taking the time to do complete background checks. The advantage of using social media sites for pre-screening is their ability to retrieve information on potential employees from as far back as high school. Sometimes past employments that were not disclosed surface. Often in such cases, the candidate has left that particular job under questionable circumstances and this should raise red flags for the recruiter. Occasionally, recruiters using various social media sites will find contradictory resumes from the same candidate.

Some searches may reveal more-troubling information than just omitted job positions. I recently read about a recruiter discovering a drunk-driving conviction that appeared in a police blotter on a local newspaper's website. When the candidate was asked about the conviction, they confirmed it and then removed themselves from the candidate list. It is however, important to remember that not everything on the internet is fact. Questionable allegations should lead the recruiter to ask certain questions and do additional research. Whether you use traditional or social media recruiting, it's imperative that thorough reference checking be done.

Is your organization ready for social media recruiting?

Given the fact that there are hundreds of millions of social media site users it is very easy and lightning fast to establish a pool of potential applicants. Search on LinkedIn and you will find hundreds that match the exact profile you are looking for. Or turn to Twitter for anybody discussing a specific keyword and now you have hundreds more to contact. But with only a set number of hours in a day, there just is not the bandwidth to contact everybody. This reality is a mixed blessing, it really depends if your organization is ready for social media recruiting or not. If you are ready then it's a huge opportunity to have the luxury of connecting with so many passive seekers. If you are not ready then you are being over-burdened by too much choice and not enough resources to sort through the masses of online profiles.

"The key to attracting the right employees and customers using social media is to provide social platforms and opportunities for all stakeholders to have a conversation, create content and help reinforce the brand through ongoing dialogue between staff, future hires and the community as a whole" - Shane Gibson, co-author of the book *Sociable!* The starting point is to identify the networks used by your target audience and get involved. If there isn't a network that caters to them, then this may provide you and your organization an opportunity to take a leadership role to create a platform like this. Monster.com saw this opportunity and created SalesHQ.com, a portal specifically for sales professionals that now boasts over 100,000 sales people and sales managers on

their mailing list.
Social media has a low cost of entry
Organizations that use Web 2.0 technologies can choose from a host of low-cost, high impact options to build their brand and connect with candidates online. Starting a blog or creating a Facebook page is simple, requires minimal resources to start-up or maintain, and helps an organization build a talent pipeline by establishing company-specific groups and committees.

Different networks appeal to different demographics
Part of a successful recruiting strategy is utilizing the networks that are relevant to the target audience. For example, organizations looking to hire recent college graduates may want to focus more heavily on Facebook, while organizations seeking a mid-career professional may have better results using LinkedIn. You need to know where your target market hangs out, establish a profile and facilitate conversations. The key to success with social networking is to understand that each site appeals to different demographics. Companies need to ensure they have consistent brand messaging across the various networks they participate in, yet still ensure their contribution to the community is relevant.

Building brand equity is driven by social behaviours
Embracing a social media strategy requires a shift in mindset. In the past, recruiters were solely associated with their organization. Today, social networks require organizations to associate themselves with their people. For recruiters, this means demonstrating thought leadership on behalf of the organization, building trust and creating personal connections with members of a targeted community.

"The Four C's": Communication, Collaboration, Conversation and Community

Social networks foster communities where people tend to gather around a common goal or shared interest and interact regularly. Join the conversation, but remember that as a member of the community, you need to do a fair share of listening. Engage in conversations with community members, share ideas and actively participate. Recruiters should be transparent about their connection to their company because contributing towards an authentic brand is one of the most crucial pieces to online success.

Candidates want to know that the recruiter can be trusted in guiding their career to the next step, and as the recruiter becomes active in the community, it encourages candidates to accept further recruitment invitations. While joining communities and participating in groups is valuable to connecting with candidates, creating a group can also help recruiters reach a relevant and defined audience. As a group owner, organizations can take advantage of access to members and their contact information.

Perhaps they're interested in candidates with a certain set of skills or experience at a particular employer— by creating their own group, companies can develop relationships with people who are likely to fit their recruiting needs.

Social networking can provide a greater depth of information about candidates and granular insight into target companies

On social networks like LinkedIn and Facebook, users create profiles that include their contact information, employment history, hobbies, association memberships and network connections. This enables recruiters to conduct more targeted searches when looking for a candidate. Understanding who the "movers and shakers" are in a target company, who has received recent promotions, and, even more importantly, the inner makeup of the company's demographics, will undoubtedly result in a robust strategy to attract top talent.

Targeted searches reduce cycle time

Once companies have created or joined a collaborative community, they'll be able to gain rapid access to a community of people with the right skills and qualifications. Traditionally, recruiters don't start the recruiting process until a requisition opens. With social networking, recruiters utilize scalable relationships to quickly meet business demands—creating transparent and proactive recruiting efforts.

There's no denying the current cultural shift happening in recruiting. Web 2.0 is having a serious impact on the business world, and progressive organizations that admire creativity and forward-thinking top talent need to utilize their recruiting teams wisely.

Follow that trail, it always leads you somewhere

By studying a trail you can learn a lot about both the destination and the journey of getting there. By looking at an individual's social media trail the employer can quickly gain valuable insights to where they started from, what's their current location and where they are heading. When reviewing online profiles people that look like stronger candidates to approach generally are the ones who:

- Has multiple recommendations from clients, peers, managers and colleagues
- Has a complete profile
- Is an active member of professional associations
- Has a work appropriate picture
- Lists non work related interests and hobbies
- Gives back by volunteering
- Updates their status more often than others
- Asks and answers more questions
- Links to their employer, blog and other projects of interest
- Has a large network

On LinkedIn:

Recommendations for Denis

Top qualities: Great Results, Expert, Good Value

> **President**
> **Dr. Denis Cauvier Seminars International**
>
> *"Denis provided Alberta Agriculture with excellent tools to assist small and medium sized businesses with recruitment and retention strategies. He also provided an entire toolkit that could be easily implemented in a human resource department which would provide all the necessary tools and documents to hire and manage employees. He is extremely knowledgeable and definitely exceeded my expectations." November 19, 2009*

On their blog:

- Has interesting points about their profession and industry
- Updates with new posts regularly
- Provides useful insights or tips that can help others
- Is genuine and honest and doesn't use blog to hard sell
- Share insights into their life outside of work – family, friends, hobbies, etc. without relaying confidential or embarrassing information
- Never knocks the competition, current or previous employer or co-workers
- Provides links to their other social networking profiles
- Includes a link to their current resume
- Avoids controversial topics such as sex, politics, religion
- Has a blogroll with link to other interesting blogs

On Facebook:

- Balances appropriately their personal and professional lives
- Posts appropriate pictures of friends and family
- Updates often
- Is an active member of professional associations
- Avoids controversial topics such as sex, politics, religion

On Twitter:

- Posts intelligent thoughts not random ramblings
- Tweets often, but not obsessively (4-16 times/ day)
- Doesn't just update, but also responds to others
- Keeps a healthy balance between personal and professional tweets
- Has a healthy followers/following ratio
- Has a large network
- Demonstrates knowledge and insight by sharing valuable content
- Promotes other people and ideas within the Twitter community

On Google:

- Doesn't come up blank
- Is the correct person
- Does not lead to something controversial like arrests, or secret lifestyle; or to an inappropriate site
- Leads to profession-related discussions and commentary on other social media sites
- Leads to their online blog, webpage or social media profiles

Here is the all important question, if somebody has the skills that an employer requires, why are all of the above criteria important? The short answer is that nowadays employers rarely hire just skills and are looking for much more of a complete package – skills, plus a well-rounded individual that fits well with their team and company. A person's social media trail gives recruiters the best insight into that person's passions, interests, communication styles, work habits, work/life balance and all sorts of other valuable information. In addition to this more and more of our customers and staff see social networks and media as a primary communication and organizational tool. Your staff must not just use social media and social networking but must be savvy enough to be able to engage your stakeholders effectively with these tools.

follow us on twitter

Twitter has been referred as "Blogging on Crack"

Twitterer Janis Krums is on a ferry in the Hudson as US Airways flight 1549 goes down & posts this photo from his iphone. - 34 minutes later Krums is interviewed live on MSNBC as an eyewitness.

 jkrums

Follow

http://twitpic.com/135xa – There's a plane in the Hudson. I'm on the ferry going to pick up the people. Crazy.

Lip-dubbing

One of the newest methods to attract young talent is to use the hugely popular YouTube website to host creative recruiting videos. In these videos teams perform little skits showcasing a "typical day" at the office. Done as choreographed, lip-sync to an overdubbed hit song, usually shot on a home digital video camera. These less than-broadcast quality videos are getting millions of hits and resulting in hundreds of resumes from talented people who would love to be part of such a fun-loving organization. There is also a dedicated site for these lip-dubs, officelipdub.com.

My long time friend and colleague, Shane Gibson recently co-authored the book *Sociable!* with Stephen Jagger. Stephen has an innovative way to recruit talent from half way around the world at www.OutsourcingThingsDone.com. They lease skilled team members from developing countries to North American small and medium sized businesses. They take the time to understand all parties needs to ensure there is a correct fit. They maximize the probability of long term success by training the client and leased team member with their proprietary systems and methodologies.

To see an example of how a client records a video message to potential team members/applicants go to:- http://video.combustionlabs.com/v/45-jobsmyotd/Spectrum-Skate-Boards

To see the selected team member record a video message introducing themselves go to: http://video.combustionlabs.com/v/45-jobsmyotd/Executive-Assistant-Davy-De-Borja

To see how to attract applicants by posting help wanted ads in a unique manner go to: http://video.combustionlabs.com/v/45-jobsmyotd/Do-you-have-Bookkeeping-Chops-

It's about Contributing Directly to the Conversation

The Obama campaign of 2008 is widely credited for its unprecedented use of new media for everything from fundraising to volunteer recruitment and coordination. The combination of an unwavering strategic vision and the collaborative technologies including blogs, social networks, twitter and SMS messaging empowered a formidable online community to elect the world's first "digital" President. It is often said that "money talks" consider the powerful story that this tells. In comparing fundraising results McCain's camp raised a total of $360 million of which $75 million was generated online, while Obama's camp amassed $750 million of which a staggering $500 million was raised online. The world's first "digital" President didn't stop connecting via social networking upon being sworn in, in fact one minute after President Obama took the office, whitehouse.gov was relaunched with a blog on the homepage.

10 Best Practices for Using Social Media Recruiting

Social Media works because it humanizes your company, engaging your audience in a more direct way than with other recruiting mediums.

Here are some tips to think about as you analyze the social media aspect of your recruitment strategy:

1. **Set a goal:** Setting a strategy before implementing tactics is critical to any business initiative. Before you dabble in social media, ask yourself if branding and awareness, client lead generation, candidate pipelining, candidate or client communication, or employee engagement is your aim.

2. **Master one medium at a time:** Many companies believe social media is an all or nothing adventure. However, the best approach is to start with one site. Head to your top pick and get comfortable with the interface and its unique features. It takes time and dedication to plan and follow through on posting new materials, developing a user base, etc. Once you are comfortable with that tool begin to add new social media tools to the mix. Redundancy will increase the number of opportunities to engage and will also help you increase your reach.

3. **Manage your online reputation:** Social media is all about word-of-mouth marketing. Share success stories, from an employee's perspective, about working with your organization. Highlight your unique knowledge and share useful information with candidates that they will share with others.

4. **Create a user experience:** Social media is about creating an open dialogue and building relationships with others, with the end goal of creating an active community. You don't want one-hit wonders; you want to start conversations that engage your audience and keep them coming back for more.

5. **Listen, learn and engage:** The most important thing you can do on any site is to listen to your audience. The second most important step is to digest that information and then respond. As you build trust with your community, you will be able to engage talent in candid discussions about your company and value.

6. **Highlight specific jobs:** Posting all your openings on social media is great, but it is more effective to focus on specific openings each week or even month. Give more than just a job posting; provide talent unique information about the company or job. Help candidates understand why the job might be the right opportunity.

7. **Visually stimulate:** From simple photos and videos to fancy custom applications, get your audience visually stimulated and you will get their attention. Incorporate photos and videos in everything you do. You want your company to stand out and interesting multimedia content is the best way to get attention.

8. **Boost your rankings:** Adding your presence to social media sites will organically boost your online profile in search rankings. Search engines count links from well known sites and blogs as votes. The more votes from high authority sites the higher your search engine ranking." Thus, by associating your company with a popular social media site, it can improve where you come up in search results.

9. **Prepare to change:** Social media is the cool new "thing" on the Internet. However, no one platform is poised to become the end-all-be-all of social media or even social media recruitment at this point in time. The hot site next month may not even be on anyone's radar, yet. Be on the lookout for new sites and don't be afraid to test the waters.

10. **Promotion:** Promote your presence once you are up and running on the social media platforms of your choice. Place links on your web site, put them in your email signature, highlight them in marketing campaigns, and even send links to become fans, friends, or followers in application confirmation emails.

Source: CareerBuilder.com

10 Commandments to Getting Started

By now the benefits of engaging in Hired 2.0 social media recruiting should be evident. But try to launch a strong social networking recruiting strategy without adequate planning and preparation, or miss a critical element along the way, and very quickly your candidate pools can dry up as top talent grows tired of waiting for your response or moves on to a better functioning recruitment process. The recruiter who is better prepared to handle the increase in response, and to deliver consistent quality employer branding messages to passive job seekers wins. At this point I am making the following assumptions; that your senior leadership team already understands and is committed to the principles of Hired 2.0, and that your organization currently and in the future will invest the majority of its resources to fulfilling the 10 key employee experiences.

1. Thou Shall Assign a Guardian of your Hired 2.0 Activities

Determine who your company's "go-to person" will be for social media recruiting, this person will take responsibility for your Hired 2.0 activities. They will need to liaise with the people responsible for all of your company's online goals from marketing to e-commerce. Ideally, your Hired 2.0 guardian should be a part of your senior leadership team. This person should possess not only a clear grasp of your goals and objectives, but they will also demonstrate a working technological knowledge of the social media marketplace tools or know how to outsource to achieve your objectives. If not already established, intellectual property policies and wide-range social media procedures should be established and well-communicated with all parties before going live and ensure that your strategic management, Human Resources and legal counsel teams are all on board. Specifying these before a problem arises will be well worth the extra time and effort, preventing potentially detrimental or costly litigation in the future.

Sample Job Description: Social Media Recruiter

Responsibilities:

- Drive a high-level of traffic to micro websites optimized for key roles, track submittals and resulting hires.
- Serves as the primary point of contact and evangelizes, promotes and drives social media programs to maintain external enthusiasm around Company X.
- Measures and communicates the impact of web community/social media strategies and tactics using agreed upon tracking metrics.
- Researches, analyzes and monitors financial, technological, and demographic factors in order to capitalize on recruiting opportunities and minimize the effects of competitive activity.
- Monitors and moderates community participation on blogs and forums sponsored by Company X and ensures prompt responses when needed.
- Contributes towards promotion activities specifically linked to Company X's web presence, such as contests, tours, and seminars.
- Represents Company X at various conferences to evangelize Company X to passive prospects and active jobseekers
- Serve as an expert in any and all online content – forums, blogs, discussion sites – to help reach targeted passive prospects.
- Lead internal effort to recruit, train and oversee existing employee involvement in Social Media for the purpose of integrating said effort into the existing Employee Referral Program.
- Prepares reports, including charts and graphs, and presents recommendations for workforce action plans to management.

Requirements:

- 5 years of online research, community management and/or marketing experience, with minimum 3 years experience in social media
- Experience working remotely with a dynamic, global team.
- Exceptional planning skills
- Self-motivated
- Ability to set realistic, measurable goals
- Ability to adjust goals according to weekly data analysis
- Experience operating in a start-up environment

2. Thou Shall Establish an Effective Website

Establish your organization's online identity via your website. If your website is not already functional or is lacking in content or visible appeal, for the most professional appearance this may require outsourcing to a reputable firm or assignment to your in-house development team. Since brand re-enforcement starts at home(page), your website is a logical place to incorporate new recruiting efforts. Branding should be consistent throughout every possible touch-point, so if your "Careers" page differs significantly in feel or layout from your other web pages, seekers will sense a disconnect. Maintain your company logo and colour schemes throughout, restate your core company values or vision statements on your career page, and include other brand-consistent messages and information sidebars.

Online visitors should always be able to see a "Careers" link easily on the home page without having to search for it. Research indicates that if the visitor must make more than three clicks to find what they want, most will move on and go elsewhere. Having a simple "Careers" or "Employment" tab or button directly on the home page, which links to a more detailed and seeker-focused Career Opportunities page will do. Once on the Careers page, visitors should be able to quickly locate clear information on current job openings and instructions on how to inquire. If the firm has very few available openings, consider a generic "We're always interested in talking to future teammates" type of message, to encourage potentially passive seekers to keep you in mind and promote future sourcing. A one line, "We are not hiring" message can deliver the equivalent of a slammed door, and it can make your entire organization appear cold or unapproachable.

3. Thou Shall Become Sociable

Replicate your identity in the social media universe by opening user accounts on Facebook, MySpace, Twitter, LinkedIn, YouTube, and any other relevant media sites. If you already have a few of these established, try to unify your various media in appearance as much as practical so that your branding is consistent. Visitors who connect with you in one marketplace should begin to associate a unified image as they connect in other means. If you have one or two social media accounts already and you'll need to create new accounts on other media sites to expand your reach, choose user account names that are the same as (or the most closely similar to) your main website name to be consistent in your branding efforts. If all of these social media accounts are new for you, it may be worthwhile to search each of the social markets for the username you prefer to use, in case it's already in use. If your organization's name is somewhat common, you may need to be creative in developing a simple but unique username which will associate visitors with your image and industry. Keeping your recruiting focus in mind, consider what impression a job seeker will have when they view your online presence, and use an account name which will still be relevant a few years from now.

4. Thou Shall Welcome Strangers into Your Home

Turning your organization into a source of relevant news and information can be an ideal method of attracting passive candidates to you. Set up a news posting or blog area on your organization's website to update on a regular basis and drive regular traffic to your website, and be certain to integrate traffic counters for later measurements. Allow visitors the opportunity to post comments or responses about your articles and encourage constructive dialogue about potentially relevant subjects. Exercise caution in open forums; so that you may properly manage the content of comments posted to your blog and help control spam or blog trolls, your comment sections are best designed with moderator controls. Permitting comments that assert opposing viewpoints to your blog, so long as these are handled in a constructive and professional manner can provide you an opportunity to also post constructive responses. Visitors who read these dialogues can then see your willingness to hold open-minded discussions, which can result in your being viewed by potential candidates as an employer of admirable character. Another key reason to drive traffic to your site is that all the contact information you might have on a social media site is not your property, it belongs to the site, so you are vulnerable should the site close or decide to close your account, you would loose all of the contacts.

5. Thou Shall Embrace the Magic Orange Icon

Whether referred to as "Rich Site Summary" or "Real Simple Syndication", RSS functionality allows the posters of news content (you) to push out their news updates to subscribers (readers) based upon keywords or specific subscription. In a way it functions similar to a GPS locator by directing readers to various news stories of interest with little effort on their part. Set up an RSS feed link of your news page or blog feed to allow visitors to receive instant notification of updates to your content. An RSS feed will syndicate your content out to your connections without their having to remember to check back on your site for updates and when your news content contains keywords that reference possible hiring or growth opportunities increased interest from the passive candidate pool is almost a certainty. Most blog creation tools will include an RSS activation feature.

6. Thou Shall Map Out the Trail

In the same manner that a map legend provides keys for understanding a map's contents, your web pages should also provide visitors with a legend of where else to find and follow you. Add the affiliated social media icons to your home page footers to advertise your online connections and let visitors know how to connect with you away from your website. Include these icon links on your regular outgoing email by adding them to the default email signature footers. If you're partnered with association groups in your industry, investigate cross-link opportunities with these organizations and explore the options of sharing partner endorsements in exchange for active site links. There may also be online groups within local chapters of national associations within your niche or industry. These all offer further opportunities to drive passive seekers to your site as you share your bulletins and maintain dialogue on industry topics.

7. Thou Shall TWEET YOUR HORN!

Don't play shy, post your news stories. On your website news page or blog, post newsworthy articles about current events within your organization, or issue pertinent opinions or editorials about industry-specific trends or national stories. The goal is to drive traffic back to your website, not to make a sales pitch and valuable industry-specific posts can attract the interest of those difficult-to-reach passive job seekers. Search for newsworthy data sources, and subscribe yourself to receive Google alerts on everything from industry legislative updates to local Chamber of Commerce information. Keeping your blog content fresh and timely will continue to drive additional traffic to your site. Then repost your own news stories out to your various other mediums. Using your Twitter account, tweet a one-line teaser comment with the URL linking back to your blog, and post the first paragraph of your blog article in your social media outlets with a link back to the full article. Odds are excellent that your company has something newsworthy to share, at least on a monthly basis and opportunities for news posts are almost limitless. Your organization's community service recognition award, your marketing department's quality in advertising honour, or employee accomplishments such as educational designations or milestones are all excellent topics for news posts. Even your corporate events, such as hosting a major client function or educational seminar are also opportune subjects for broadcasting. These posts increase awareness of your presence to both passive candidates and potential customers.

8. Thou Shall Maximize Your Casting

Maximize your search engines and turn them into passive candidate recruitment tools. In Google Advanced search, you can search within LinkedIn for a Call Center Manager in Atlanta and the resulting search parameters (Atlanta "call center manager" site:linkedin.com) can yield hundreds of registered LinkedIn connection results to which you can send individual LinkedIn connection invitations or "In-Mail." Try the same type of search with other networking sites such as Spoke or Facebook to cast an even wider passive candidate net.

9. Thou Shall Assume the Role of Professor

Successful and proactive workers are continuously on the lookout for educational opportunities, especially those individuals with designations or continuing educational credit requirements. Engage the passive seekers within your industry by offering regular educational options. If professionals in your trade require CE credits, become a reputable news alert outlet for informing the public about locally available resources to meet these requirements. For an even more effective and personal connection, arrange and host credit-hour certified educational courses within your own facility or offer certified credit hours through live video webcast opportunities via tools such as WebEx, LiveMeeting, or GoToMeeting. Then take advantage of your news posting outlets to advertise these offerings. And since your course offerings will require individual registrations, your passive candidate list will also benefit by your recording and storing the valuable contact information of your course attendees. To ensure that your educational options will provide the promised CE hours, confer with the designated licensing or certification authority before scheduling or announcing the event.

10. Thou Shall Learn From the Past

Without accurate feedback and intentional study of your social media expeditions, identification of what activities did or did not succeed will be difficult at best. Measure the effectiveness of your Hired 2.0 elements by reviewing your site counters, blog comments and responses and solicit feedback from trusted staff and impartial colleagues about how your efforts may be improved or refined. Regular benchmarking of your passive candidate flow before activating a new social recruiting element can also help to identify which sources and methods resulted in higher numbers of new connections and which ones yielded undesirable results or no tangible results at all.

Adapted from: A Recruiters Field Guide, BrightMove, Inc.

Organizations that have hired exceptional talent using social media recruiting

Dell Computers - has a squad of 42 employees who spend their workdays engaging with the communities on Facebook, Twitter, and other social media with specific focus on customer contact, overall brand building/reinforcement and recruiting of talent

Zappos.com lead by C.E.O. Tony Hsieh is an online retailer success story that sells shoes, clothing and accessories. The people at Zappos truly understand new media networking and have used social media marketing to explode their sales and create a global brand. They have leverage this way of thinking to include employee engagement and social recruiting. There is a dedicated page for Twitter on its homepage that's linked to from every other page on the site with the words "What are Zappos employees doing right now?" All 198 of its employees are on Twitter. They have effectively created a squad of 198 recruiters that are directly linked into like minded people around the world.

Harvard Business Publishing boss Alexandra Samuel recently shared his experience on how he was able to hire his newest member Channing Rodman with social media. Channing was hired as a Social Media Strategist and she has according to Samuel "rocked our world with her terrific online instincts, brilliant writing and client diplomacy."

As is the case with most small organizations, each needs to be multitasked. They prioritize the core competencies, skills, knowledge areas and personality attributes they were looking for in the ideal person. They posted a comprehensive job description on their web site, and a shorter version was posted on Craigslist. They then twittered the link, the near immediate result was a huge volume of retweets, link love and site visits. Channing's brother, Sean saw -- and forwarded -- the job posting to his sister. Sean and Channing co-author the Social Ch@nge blog, so he knew exactly how much the position would interest her. Channing wasn't the only talented social media professional they connected with as a result of this online recruitment process. They connected with several other bloggers, strategists and project managers who they are likely to work with on future projects as contractors.

Although Channing's applicant, resume and cover letter were all very compelling, the fact that she was living in Poland presented a challenge in that the selection committee had to be 100% confident with the prescreening process prior to having someone move half-way across the world for the position. The next step was to have a brief phone call that confirmed that yes, she sounded like a serious candidate. With every screening call, Samuel would put my notes in a special file on the company share drive that would be accessible to any of the selection committee. The first interview took place via Skype video: having experience conducting video meetings with clients provide the selection committee a good sense of how someone's on-screen presence corresponds to their real-life personality. Channing won them over with her warm, polished, and effective answering of tough questions; she even had the confidence and poise to challenge the selection committee on a scenario they had created to gauge candidate's comfort levels when working with questionable clients. Additional Skype meetings were conducted with other key members of the team, and with their business coach. They wrapped up the screening process by conducting references checks by phone. The selection team recognized the long distance wasn't just a challenge for them; the time it took to prescreen made for a long (and anxiety-producing) hiring process for Channing. They felt that the regular emails, IM and the video interviews provided critical check-ins that kept her engaged in the process and helping both parties build a relationship. The hiring of Channing has worked out very well. Samuel says, "Our clients love working with her; so do our development partners and staff. Her social media instincts, creativity and solid project management skills have all exceeded our admittedly high expectations".

Boston Staffing Firm Hollister

Hollister is a Boston-based, woman-owned, full-service staffing firm that has recently launched "Recruiting 2.0", a social media platform that uses Web 2.0 technologies (LinkedIn, Twitter, Facebook, etc) to discover the best job candidates for clients. For Hollister, using social networks is an effective way to position clients' job opportunities in front of active and passive candidates, discover new talent, and acquire in-depth information about candidates.

"Recruiting 2.0 complements our traditional recruiting efforts and enhances our ability to consistently identify the most talented professionals for our clients," explains Kip Hollister, Founder and CEO of Hollister. Hollister's recruiters are able to position their clients' job opportunities in front of both active and sought-after passive job candidates.

Recruiting 2.0 comprises an array of organically fed online networking communities on Twitter, LinkedIn and Facebook, spanning each of Hollister's staffing areas: Accounting & Finance; Sales; Administrative; Creative & Marketing; Human Resources; and Technology. In addition to these forums, Hollister provides value to clients by managing three widely read blogs: The Boston Hiring Blog, The Boston Jobs Blog, and The Boston Networking Blog. What makes this 2.0 model unique is its ability to reach both active job-seekers, as well as more passive candidates who would otherwise be difficult to engage and who are less likely to utilize online job boards. Through the model, Hollister recruiters are given a more complete picture of job candidates than they would gain from traditional resumes alone.

"I believe that most recruiting firms will eventually fully embrace social media," remarked Hollister. "We are happy to have wrapped our arms around this early on in the game, so that we can continue to remain competitive in serving our clients' recruitment needs."

JobsBoston

1. How do I look for a job while I have a job? Beat the Interview Flu - http://ow.ly/x8K612:51 PM Oct 28th from HootSuite

2. HOT JOB! Executive Assistant to the Office of the Dean needed for a top University, Apply Here: http://ow.ly/x8gb #bostonjobs12:31 PM Oct 28th from HootSuite

3. What Job Seekers Need to Know About Google: http://ow.ly/x8wd12:16 PM Oct 28th from HootSuite

4. Senior Interactive Designer needed in Boston. 8-10 years relevant experience w/ strong portfolio... http://ow.ly/x86j #bostonjobs12:03 PM Oct 28th from HootSuite

5. HOT JOB! Recruiting Coordinator to work at prominent organization in the Boston Area: Apply NOW! http://ow.ly/x88o #bostonjobs11:50 AM Oct 28th from HootSuite

6. Resume Recasts Bookkeeper as HR Powerhouse - http://ow.ly/x8uS11:46 AM Oct 28th from HootSuite

7. Web Production Artist needed in Metro Boston. Photoshop exp needed, Dreamweaver & Flash knowledge a plus! http://ow.ly/x85J #bostonjobs11:26 AM Oct 28th from HootSuite

8. Q&A - Using LinkedIn for Job References - http://ow.ly/x8t211:21 AM Oct 28th from HootSuite

9. Chargemaster position open for experienced Medical Billing Supervisor - Knowledge of CPT/HCPCS coding needed - http://ow.ly/x83P #bostonjobs11:11 AM Oct 28th from HootSuite

10. Financial Analyst needed in Beverly w/ 4+ yrs FP&A experience w/in a large company & expert Excel skills - http://ow.ly/x83l #bostonjobs10:50 AM Oct 28th from HootSuite

11. Looking for a New Job? Follow the Pink Slips - http://ow.ly/x8s710:46 AM Oct 28th from HootSuite

12. HOT JOB! Executive Assistant to COO for an outstanding Cambridge international Non-Profit health organization: http://ow.ly/x8fD #bostonjobs10:32 AM Oct 28th from HootSuite

13. Storage Engineer job in Natick, MA. 2-5 yrs Storage experience, 5 yrs Unix Sys admin. Apply now: http://ow.ly/x81H #bostonjobs10:32 AM Oct 28th from HootSuite

14. Using Creativity to Stand Out in Your Career - via WSJ: http://ow.ly/x8rB10:13 AM Oct 28th from HootSuite

15. MARKETING MANAGER JOB in Metro Boston. Preferred technical skill set (PowerPoint, Photoshop...), 3-5 yrs exp. http://ow.ly/x8ds #bostonjobs9:58 AM Oct 28th from HootSuite

16. .NET Developer needed w/ 3+ yrs .NET experience. Learn more and apply today! http://ow.ly/x7WI #bostonjobs9:40 AM Oct 28th from HootSuite

17. Avoid laundry list resumes. Learn how now! http://ow.ly/x6fE7:54 AM Oct 28th from HootSuite

18. Read about what to do when you haven't heard back from an employer after sending out your resume/cover letter! GREAT TIPS! http://ow.ly/x6ap7:50 AM Oct 28th from HootSuite

19. Attention ladies! Learn how to avoid the ways that women can sabotage their jobs! Read more @ http://ow.ly/x62A7:44 AM Oct 28th from HootSuite

20. Read about Microsoft's new Windows 7 launch, including its new perks today! http://ow.ly/x4F06:25 AM Oct 28th from HootSuite

Recruiting Lawyers via Facebook

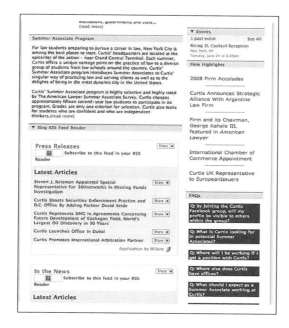

LAUNCHSQUAD.

While searching Twitter for comments about his clients, San Francisco PR entrepreneur Jason Throckmorton noticed a post from a University of Oregon undergraduate. Searching further, he found a blog from the same student discussing how the PR industry was evolving. "We said, 'This is the kind of person we're interested in,'" says Throckmorton, 34. The co-founder of $5 million LaunchSquad contacted the student, invited her to visit and wound up adding her to his staff of 35.

marcel|media
Full-service online + interactive marketing firm

Ben Swartz, co-founder and president of Chicago-based interactive marketing advisory firm Marcel Media, estimates he's hired three-quarters of his 21-person staff using Hired 2.0. He uses LinkedIn and Facebook to learn about candidates in depth. "In a typical resume, you might get a line on interests, on LinkedIn, you can find out who they associate with. On Facebook, you might find some groups and associations and even pictures. It gives us more dimensions than a static resume can offer."

Referrals can work if employers encourage employees to post information about job duties and corporate culture. If your employees are your biggest assets, why not leverage them to help you differentiate your company and attract and recruit future talent? Bearing this in mind Swartz urges employees to create blog entries about Marcel Media, which earns more than $3 million in annual sales, plastering the company Web site with employee comments and even placing podcasts of company news on the Web site.

BETA
Jobirn

InsidersReferral.com Inc.'s job site Jobirn (jobirn.com) connects candidates, employers, and recruiters via IM rather than conventional but slower email. Bruce Ge, founder and CEO says," A lot of deals should be done interactively, instead of sending emails, they should send instant messages."

TheCareerMole.com sets up a channel for current employees to mentor candidates and provide information about company culture and jobs. "Opening new lines of communication between potential candidates and small companies has a significant impact on candidate experience and conversion rates," says director Oliver Perry. Candidates who know what's expected of them and what life in the company might really be like tend to be easier to hire and perform better.

Better Work Stories - BBQ

The New Zealand Police Force understands that one of the key components of successful recruiting messages is to stand out from the crowd of most messages and grab the attention of passive job seekers. They have been successful at doing this with a very reasonable budget. They created a series of short TV style ads that have small groups of friends together in various social settings; the sports game, the bar, the backyard BBQ. Each short video has a common theme, "Better Work Stories". In each video you have one of the characters trying in vain to explain a "cool" event that happened that day at work. In reality the friends are bored with the story and see the job as lame. The final few seconds shows an action packed collage of snippets from a typical day as a member of the Police Force. These videos are very funny and they have captured the imagination of hundreds of excellent young men and women to apply to the force. What I really like about this campaign is that no expensive TV ad time was purchased all the videos are up loaded to YouTube and then shared around the world by over 6,000 viewers.

When facing some recent challenges to recruiting new police officers the LA Police Department decided to capitalize on one of Los Angles best assets and create a social media recruitment blitz. Recruitment film "trailers" that were Hollywood produced. These quickly cut, and musically driven, trailers showed an LAPD officers typical 12 hour day fighting crime and helping citizens all around Los Angeles in some of the City's most recognizable spots from the 6th Street Bridge downtown to the boardwalk in Venice. The trailers first appeared on the newly redesigned www.JoinLAPD.com website, the campaign was also supported with billboards, radio ads featuring live sound from the films, and movie theatres screened the trailers before live movies. The trailers were also uploaded to YouTube and there it went viral.

Journey Gets In-Sync with Social Media Recruiting

One of the most successful bands of the eighties Journey has had some challenges in finding and keeping lead singers since the legendary Steve Perry left the band in 1996 to focus on his solo career. Since Perry's departure the band has gone through five lead singers. After trying multiple traditional approaches to hire the sixth lead vocals, including running ads for tryouts in various music industry magazines a friend of Journey member Neil Schon alerted him to a YouTube video of Arnel Pineda, a Philippines singer who could barely speak a word of English. Pineda's video showed with his band called the Zoo belting out the iconic "Don't Stop Believin'. Schon was so impressed with the vocals that Pineda was flown to California for a live tryout and to see if he would gel with the band. As Schon said in a press release: "After watching Arnel's videos over and over again, I had to walk away from the computer and let what I heard sink in because it sounded too good to be true. I thought, 'he can't be that good.' But he is that good, he's the real deal and so tremendously talented. Arnel doesn't sound synthetic and he's not emulating anyone. I tried to get a hold of him through YouTube and I finally heard from him that night, but it took some convincing to get him to believe that it really was me and not an imposter." Arnel, was hired and his first major test was in front of more than 80,000 fans in Brazil, the audience loved the newest addition to the band, and the team still rocks on!

follow us on twitter

Starbucks is Hiring: store manager - Manhattan (New York, NY). Apply via this link: http://bit.ly/1iJciK - Please RT. #jobs #starbucks12:47 PM Oct 9th from web

CIA Gets in Your Face(book)

Since December 2006, the Central Intelligence Agency has been using Facebook.com, to recruit potential employees into its National Clandestine Service. It marks the first time the CIA has ventured into social networking to hire new personnel. The CIA's Facebook page (login required) provides an overview of what the NCS is looking for in a recruit, along with a 30-second promotional YouTube video aimed at potential college-aged applicants. U.S. citizens with a GPA above 3.0 can apply.

"It's an invaluable tool when it comes to peer-to-peer marketing," says Michele Neff, a CIA spokeswoman.

U.S. Coast Guard Channel on YouTube: From the Red River floods that ravaged North Dakota to the "Miracle on the Hudson" emergency landing, the U.S. Coast Guard plays a critical role in responding to the needs of fellow Americans in moments of crisis. You might see a sound bite of their heroic efforts on TV, but you can also catch the Coast Guard in action any time on YouTube. Travel with Commandant Allen, who has mandated social media as a vital part of the Coast Guard mission, or catch fearless Coasties conducting safety checks by airboat, rescuing stranded citizens from swelling rivers, and saving lives in stormy seas.

State Department DipNote Blog: While all State Department employees aren't engaged in espionage or excursions to exotic locales, you can get a flavour for the foreign service as a regular reader of the State Department's DipNote blog. Several recent posts feature photos from the Global Women's Mentoring Partnership and an account of U.S. Ambassador Stephen Nolan launching a solar energy project at Kaziikini Campsite in Botswana. Young women looking for opportunities to have a global impact or a students seeking "green" employment, would likely find these posts quite appealing. In fact these posts are so appealing that DipNote has had more than 5,000,000 page views.

UK Training and Development Agency for Schools (TDA) on Facebook: The United Kingdom has found Facebook to be a helpful recruitment tool for teachers. Elizabeth Doyle and Kaol Rasarathnam who partnered with the (TDA), and created two complementary Facebook pages where 2,000 fans are finding information about careers in teaching. Each site features 10 teachers and teaching career advisors who are available to answer questions that range from "What are the main software packages used by students in secondary schools?" to "I have an interview at Cambridge University for secondary biology teaching – any last-minute interview tips?" Each question is attempted to be answered within 24 hours with an average of 2-3 questions per day.

Shane Gibson and Stephen Jagger's *Sociable!* Code of Engagement

1. Treat every action as if it will be recorded for eternity

Almost everything we say online is recorded, logged and backed up somewhere. In every restaurant, bar or conference room, there are dozens of people with mobile video, photo, and blogging apps that capture our behaviour in an instant, ready to broadcast it to the world instantly and permanently. You can't delete a bad blog post, a rude response. Be careful what you say, blog, tweet and do, because the impact can be permanent.

2. Talk about what you know

Being Sociable! is about being a thought leader, and contributor to community being authentic and transparent. People rely on us for advice and guidance. Stating opinion as fact can hurt our reputation and it may even harm the person taking our advice. If we're wrong, you can expect to be called out on it and even embarrassed in the social media space by other bloggers or community members. Always be learning, studying and fact checking in the domains you aspire to lead, and don't exaggerate or fabricate your knowledge or the facts.

3. Get Engaged

Don't broadcast, connect. Being Sociable! is about listening, connecting, and contributing. Engagement is how we make other people feel. It's also about the lasting impact that we have on them and their success. To be Sociable! you must monitor conversations, listening to and communicating with individuals in the community in a personable and relevant way.

4. Give credit where credit is due

If you hear a great quote from someone, an interesting hypothesis or learn a new business process, make sure you give the author due credit. Just because something is not protected under copyright does not mean we can re-purpose it without giving credit. A link back to their site, a mention of them at your seminar or in your video only takes seconds. This builds the trust of everyone watching you, and they will know you are in this for more than just personal gain, and they will be Sociable! with you as well.

5. No Spam

Never send generic messages to people who have given you permission to connect. If they have added you as a connection in a social network, realize that this is not to be taken lightly. Only send information or communicate in a way that is adding value, every time. Avoid auto messages, auto blog links, or auto anything that makes people feel like a number and not a valued contact.

6. Know when to Zip it

Be conscious of private or confidential information that has been trusted to you. This means don't post it anywhere on the web. It also means don't talk about it in public, where someone else could hear or record you and post it online for the world to see. Know the difference between fact, opinion and slander and always air on the side of being legally diligent. In other words, don't post anything that could result in an unwanted court appearance.

7. This is not a video game

Some people see social media as a video game where you collect names and followers, to be presented in some sort of digital trophy case. This game is getting old fast. The real measure of someone who is legitimately Sociable! is their action and impact. Focus on quality of relationships with people. Focus on getting people to do something when they get to your blog, not on how many people visit it. Think in the term of profits made, impact created or actions caused by your Sociable! activity.

8. Be open to all feedback

The days of corporate white washing are over, so is having a dual life. Everyone now knows what your up to in this digital world that lacks privacy. People are going to go after you online on your personal blog, your corporate blog or blast you with a video or a comment on a social network. When this happens, don't hide and don't delete their comments or errors you may have made instead, engage. Customer complaints are branding opportunities and sometimes our critics are actually bold allies trying to set us straight. It's important to respond to criticism strategically, not emotionally, and to set the record straight with a correction, the facts or good old fashion customer service and apologies.

9. Digital rights

We make our living from the great ideas, content and creative works we create, market and produce. Being Sociable! means our brand is one of integrity, authenticity and transparency. We need to respect others copyright and creative works just like we would want them to do for us. Always ask permission or give attribution to other people's creations that you use, cite, or include in your work. Every photo, video, quote or audio clip we use must be posted and distributed in a way that respects and maintains the integrity of their work.

10. Be Sociable!

Being Sociable! also means not taking our self or our brand too seriously. In order to be a true Sociable! thought leader you must have fun, be passionate and contribute to the success of your clients, peers, family and community as a whole. Most importantly, we continually strive to "get real" by taking our online connections and meet them individually or as a community through events like Meetups, Tweetups, and community functions. We do this to deepen and expand relationships. Without strong Sociable! relationships we're just another marketer or salesperson making a pitch.

Source: Sociable! by Shane Gibson & Stephen Jagger – SociableBook.com

Author's note:

So much of the principles of effective recruiting stem from the tenants of marketing, customer service and consumer behaviour. It is a strategic advantage for those recruiters who master these skills. If you are to read one book on social media marketing it should be Sociable! by Shane Gibson and Stephen Jagger, it will not only help you and your teammates grow your business but the insights provided in this book dovetail perfectly with Hired 2.0. Please check out www.sociable.com to get your own copy of this fantastic resource.

A Cautionary Note

Solely relying on social media recruiting and failing to take advantage of more traditional recruitment methods can limit efforts to recruit a diverse work force. If you are interested in exploring other recruiting methods that can work in tandem with your Hired 2.0 campaign I would encourage you to get a copy of my book **101 Low Cost/High Impact Recruiting Methods**, ordering information can be found at the back of this book. Although older workers are slowly embracing social networking, their lower rates of computer knowledge and internet usage will make them harder to connect with. Ultimately, I don't see Hired 2.0 as a substitute for human recruiters and interviewers. It will not replace face-to-face conversation. It should be seen as a highly effective means to re-enforce your company's brand message while casting a wider net to find more qualified passive job seekers who have a better understanding of what you're looking for and for you to get a better understanding of who they are.

As various services enter the world of social media recruiting, it will be interesting to see what developments take place over the next few years. One exciting development is the concept referred to as "cloud recruiting." That's the ability to leverage all Web 2.0 opportunities at the same time, to focus on a specific solution... stand by!

Conclusion

Remember, as I stated at the beginning of this book, a company's brand is what other's (employees and outsiders) say it is, not what their paid advertising claims it to be. Your brand is really the culmination of all the conversations in your universe that are being held pertaining to your organization. The single biggest factor that drives these conversations is the type of service experience that each individual has with your company. As indicated by the **Recruiting Exceptional Talent from the Inside-Out** model back on page 13, and that the most important experiences start with your employees, those 10 key employee experiences will have a profound impact on staff turnover, employee engagement and levels of productivity. Intern, this will directly impact the level of SERVICE that the rest of your universe experiences. The conversations surrounding your brand, your company and your vacant jobs will happen with or without your contribution. It is your responsibility to positively influence the discussion and to capitalize on tapping into the global talent pool through "word of mouth recruiting" via social media sites at the "speed of light."

Now that you have read this book, keep referring to it as a constant source of practical information, be sure to take advantage of the numerous charts and questionnaires to ensure that you fully benefit from *Hired 2.0 - Recruiting Exceptional Talent at the Speed of Light.* Once you apply the principles covered within this book, the odds of being successful are in your favour.
Best of Success!

Dr. Denis Cauvier

If you enjoyed *Hired 2.0 – Recruiting Exceptional Talent at the Speed of Light,*you may be interested in two other of my international best-selling books:

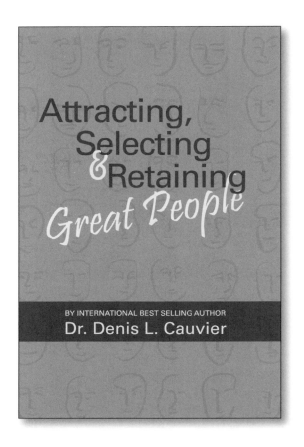

To order additional copies of the following books please refer to the order form on page 123.

Hired 2.0 – Recruiting Exceptional Talent at the Speed of Light

Attracting, Selecting & Retaining GREAT People

101 Low Cost/ High Impact Recruiting Methods

Book Order Form

Title	Quantity	Price/ book	Subtotal
Hired 2.0 – Recruiting Exceptional Talent at the Speed of Light		$24.95	
101 Low Cost/ High Impact Recruiting Methods		$24.95	
Attracting, Selecting & Retaining GREAT People		$24.95	
Please add **$4.00/book** (shipping/ handling & taxes)			
Total payment enclosed			

Please print all information clearly.

Name _____ Telephone _____

Address _____

Town_____ Province/State _____

Postal Code/ZIP _____ Telephone _____

Method of Payment

❏ Cheques or money orders accepted.

Please make payable to: **DAX Enterprises International**

Mail: DAX Enterprises International Inc.
175 Charles Street, Arnprior, Ontario K7S 3V5
Telephone: 613.623.5656
Email: dcauvier@ca.inter.net

Note: Bulk order discounts are available, please email your requirements to dcauvier@ca.inter.net

To connect with Dr. Cauvier:
www.deniscauvier.com
dcauvier@ca.inter.net
LinkedIn
Twitter
613.623.5656

Dr. Denis Cauvier Seminars International is committed to providing its clients with customized solutions tailored to their unique requirements. Practical, results-oriented training, consulting and professional speaking based solutions are available in the following areas:

- Hired 2.0: Recruiting Exceptional Talent at the Speed of Light
- How to Engage Your People & Create Strategic Advantages During Tough Economic Times
- How to Attract & Retain Exceptional Talent in Today's Labour Market
- Becoming Multi-lingual, How to Speak to & be Understood by Different Workplace Generations
- How Workplace Literacy & Essential Skills = PROFITS
- Stop Spending Money on Staff... Maximize Your Returns on People Investments
- How to Achieve Sales Results by Propelling Your Team into Action
- How to Keep Your People Productive & Happy

For more information regarding how Dr. Denis Cauvier Seminars International services can assist your organization, please contact: dcauvier@ca.inter.net • 613.623.5656.